HARP ON THE WILLOW

A play

by

John Misto

ORiGiN™
Theatrical

FOR ALL ENQUIRIES CONTACT: ORiGiN™ Theatrical
PO BOX Q1235, QVB Post Office, Sydney, NSW, 1230, Australia
Phone: (61 2) 8514 5201
enquiries@originmusic.com.au   www.origintheatrical.com.au
Part of the ORiGiN™ Music Group
An Australian Independent Music Company

IMPORTANT NOTICE

While this play may contain references to brand names or trademarks owned by third parties, or make reference to public figures, ORiGiN™ Theatrical should not be considered to be necessarily endorsing or otherwise attempting to promote an affiliation with any of the owners of the brand names or trademarks or public figures. Such references are solely for use in a dramatic context.

LANGUAGE NOTE

Licensees are welcome to make small alterations to the language that is used is this play so as to make it suitable for a younger cast and/or audience.

MUSIC USE NOTE

Licensees are solely responsible for obtaining formal written permission from copyright owners to use copyrighted music in the performance of this play and are strongly cautioned to do so. If no such permission is obtained by the licensee, then the licensee must use only original music that the licensee owns and controls. Licensees are solely responsible and liable for all music clearances and shall indemnify the copyright owners of the play(s) and their licensing agent, ORiGiN™ Theatrical, against any costs, expenses, losses and liabilities arising from the use of music by licensees. Please contact the appropriate music licensing authority in your territory for the rights to any incidental music. In Australia and New Zealand, contact APRA AMCOS apraamcos.com.au.

If you are in any doubt about any of the above then contact ORiGiN™ Theatrical.

For complete listing of plays and musicals available to perform and all licence enquiries, contact ORiGiN™ Theatrical.

www.origintheatrical.com.au
+ 61 2 8514 5201

AND HERE ARE THE RULES
IN PLAIN ENGLISH FOR YOU...

<u>DO NOT</u> perform this play without getting permission from ORiGiN™ Theatrical first. In 99% of cases you'll need to pay us money to be allowed to stage a performance. This money goes to the author(s) of the show who shed blood, sweat and tears creating this play. Please don't rob them of their livelihood.
Go online www.origintheatrical.com.au or call +61 2 8514 5201

<u>DO NOT</u> make a copy of this book by photocopying, scanning, taking a photo, retyping (on a computer or a typewriter), or using a pencil, pen or chalkboard. If you want to purchase more copies contact ORiGiN™ Theatrical.
Go online www.origintheatrical.com.au or call +61 2 8514 5201

<u>DO NOT</u> make any changes to the text without first getting permission from ORiGiN™ Theatrical in writing. Sometimes you'll be allowed to make changes and sometimes you won't. Please always check with us first.
Go online www.origintheatrical.com.au or call +61 2 8514 5201

<u>DO NOT</u> record your performances or rehearsals in anyway without first getting permission from ORiGiN™ Theatrical. We know everyone wants to try and record everything on their phones these days. We get it. But please don't encourage them or give them permission. Sometimes there are important contractual reasons as to why we can't give you permission to record it. And sometimes there aren't any reasons and we can say YES. Please just check with us first.
Go online www.origintheatrical.com.au or call +61 2 8514 5201

<u>DO</u> contact ORiGiN™ Theatrical if you have any questions about anything. At all. And we mean anything. One of us that works here (not me) has a peculiar interest in recording the unusual bird calls of the adult hoatzin (a species of tropical bird found in wet forest and mangrove of the Amazon and the Orinoco delta in South America) so we should be able to answer any questions you have about the Hoatzin. Plus we know some things about some other things too.

Thank you for taking the time to read this.

ABOUT THE AUTHOR

John Misto has been writing plays since 1992. His play, *The Shoe-Horn Sonata* has been reprinted nineteen times and sold more than sixty thousand copies. *The Shoe-Horn Sonata* also won the NSW Premier's Literary Award for Best Play and the Australia Remembers National Playwriting Prize.

Misto's other works include *Dark Voyager* about the turbulent relationship between Joan Crawford and Marilyn Monroe. Misto also wrote the hugely successful play, *Harp on the Willow* which won the Rodney Seaborn Award for Best Play. John Misto is co-writer of *Peace Train: The Cat Stevens Story* which has enjoyed several successful national tours of Australia.

John Misto's most recent play, *Lip Service* had a sell-out season at London's Park Theatre in 2017 (under the title Madame Rubinstein) and a successful season at Sydney's Ensemble Theatre and at the Lawler Theatre in Melbourne. *Lip Service* is to be performed in Poland, Lithuania and Israel.

John Misto is also an established scriptwriter and his telemovies and scripts have won many awards including the Queensland Premier's Literary Award, three Australian Film Institute Awards, three Australian Writers' Guild Awards and a Gold Plaque at the Chicago Television Awards.

John Misto has degrees in Arts and Law from the University of New South Wales.

REVIEWS

"Beautifully written...inspirational...spiked with Misto's demonically wicked good humour."
- Melbourne Stage

"Refreshing, uplifting...marvellous...a spirit of human transformation which is universally meaningful."
- Stage Whispers

"This play has everything."
- The Australian

"Harp on the Willow sublimely and comically unpacks what people do when faced with the schism between ancient tradition and a new generation's hopes...The play unfolds through a series of songs, hymns, folk tunes and feisty flashbacks...This play (is) timeless...Harp on the Willow is beautifully written."
- Paul Andrew, Australian Stage

SPECIAL THANKS

Special thank you to Mary O'Hara and John Sims for the cover photograph of Mary O'Hara which was taken in 1956 to promote Mary's appearances on BBCtv's *More Contrary* show.

For more about the life, career and music of Mary O'Hara, visit
maryohara.co.uk
maryohara-travelswithmyharp.co.uk

HARP ON THE WILLOW
Australian Premiere
Presented by Malcolm Cooke and Ensemble Productions
1 March 2007, Comedy Theatre, Melbourne
Starring: Marina Prior and Joan Carden
with Christopher Stollery, Lucy Maunder and Tom Wren

CHARACTERS

This play is inspired by real people and events.

SISTER MIRIAM PERPETUA SELIG: Early 30's, Irish, a Benedictine nun at Stanbrook Abbey in the UK. Before she entered the order, she was the famous singer Mary O'Hara.

MARY O'HARA: 19 years old, Irish, a budding fashion model who has suddenly and unexpectedly become a famous folk-singer. (Also Sister Walburga).

TYRONE KANE: 38, American, a derelict. (Also the Voice of the Priest and the Voice of the Security Guard).

MOTHER RAPHAEL WALKER: 50's, English, the Mother Superior of Stanbrook Convent. (Also the Voice of Elaine).

RICHARD SELIG: 27, American, a poet, extremely handsome. (Also the Voice of the Angry Neighbour, Voice of the Sound Engineer).

By the rivers of Babylon we sat and wept when we remembered Zion. There on the willows we hung our harps for how can we sing God's song while in a foreign land?
Psalm 137

*On the soundtrack we hear **By the Waters of Babylon** sung by Don MacLean.*

The following words are seen above the stage - "Visiting Room, Stanbrook Abbey, English Midlands, 1973".

The lights come up to reveal the Visitors' Room in Stanbrook Abbey, a Catholic convent about one hour's drive from London.

The Visitors' Room, like everything else about the convent, is truly Spartan. A wire rack displays rows of items made by the nuns which are for sale to visitors.

At the centre of the stage is a grille - (made of scrim) - ominous, impenetrable, rising like a wall.

This grille divides the visitors from the nuns. The nuns are not allowed to see their visitors. They can only talk to them.

A nun is sitting beside the grille. She is reading a prayer book. A man is standing on the other side of the grille. He is nervous, no, agitated - as some men are when they need a drink. He is barely on the right side of clean. He could shave more. He could shower more. His clothes, second-hand, have seen better days.

He gropes in his pockets for a pack of cigarettes and some matches. He shakes the match box, and takes out a match. And just as he lights the match, a voice from behind the grille says -

SISTER MIRIAM: (*Irish*) Would you do that in the garden please?

TYRONE: (*startled, looks around*) You've got to be joking. It's *freezing* out there. (*mutters*) It's freezing in *here*.

Tyrone has forgotten that he is holding a lit match - and it burns him.

TYRONE: Shit!

SISTER MIRIAM: (*more firmly*) We'd rather our guests didn't smoke inside.

TYRONE: Why? (*inhaling with exaggeration*) Because it makes people happy?

SISTER MIRIAM: Because some of the Sisters had to give up when they came here. Nicotine withdrawal on a wet Sunday night is a terrible thing to endure.

TYRONE: (*can't see anyone*) Where the hell are you, anyway?

SISTER MIRIAM: Over here. Behind the grille.

TYRONE: Well open up. I haven't got all night.

SISTER MIRIAM: I'm not *allowed* to show my face. This convent is enclosed.

TYRONE: What?

SISTER MIRIAM: Our rules do not permit us to see any of our visitors. We can only *talk* to the people who come here to ask for our help. So if you'd like this convent to pray for you, just leave a donation in the little drawer there - in front of the grille.

But Tyrone doesn't believe her.

TYRONE: (*studying the grille*) Where's your peephole?

SISTER MIRIAM: Peephole?

TYRONE: The gizmo that lets you spy on me.

SISTER MIRIAM: (*getting impatient*) I've just gone to great pains to explain it all clearly.

TYRONE: You mean you really can't see me? Not at all?

And Tyrone waves his hand across the grille, then makes a grotesque expression. As he does so -

SISTER MIRIAM: Whenever people ask me that I'm sure they pull a face.

Tyrone stops abruptly, a little unnerved. Then he takes his cigarette from his mouth and grinds it into the floor.

TYRONE: OK. I've put it out. The Marlboro I mean. So I hope you're happy.

SISTER MIRIAM: (*tersely*) Thrilled. (*slightly impatient*) Now it's late. So what can I do for you?

TYRONE: I've come for my thirty-four quid.

Tyrone takes a bottle of whisky from his pocket and has a little swig.

11

SISTER MIRIAM: We don't give money. But the monks up the road have a refuge for -

TYRONE: I'm not a beggar, sweetheart. I'm a debt-collector. From London.

SISTER MIRIAM: I thought we'd paid the bills last month. Hang on. There was one... Of course. I'm sorry. Do you mind if I ask your company's name? I'll need it for the cheque.

TYRONE: That's OK. You can pay me in cash.

SISTER MIRIAM: Cash? For the gas bill?

TYRONE: This isn't for the gas, doll. It's personal. It's a private debt. Two years ago I sent this convent a cheque for thirty-four pounds.

SISTER MIRIAM: A donation you mean?

TYRONE: No way. It was a contract. I asked you to pray for my intentions and paid you thirty-four pounds to do so. Now either you didn't try hard enough or God's packed it in and become an atheist.

SISTER MIRIAM: We don't always get what we -

TYRONE: (*sternly*) Don't try and fob me off with that *mystical* stuff. I got *nothing* for my dough. So either you pay me a refund now or I'll report this convent to the Fraud Squad.

SISTER MIRIAM: I'd better inform my Superior.

TYRONE: Your Superior? Why?

SISTER MIRIAM: She's in charge of our finances. She'll write you a cheque. For Cash of course. But she's busy now so you'll have to come back.

TYRONE: (*angrily*) Great. Just great! Another trip from London! That's all I damn-well need! Why can't you write it? Or don't you know how? I guess they use you Irish for the cooking and the cleaning.

SISTER MIRIAM: (*also angry*) With a bit of luck you'll spend our money on a plane ticket back to the Bronx. I'm sure you must be greatly missed in the bars along East 56th Street.

TYRONE: (astonished) How do you know I'm from the (*Bronx*) -

SISTER MIRIAM: None of your business. *(in a most Un-Christian way)* Go in peace!

And Sister Miriam slams the grille door shut.

Tyrone looks astonished.

SCENE TWO

*On the soundtrack we hear **Jesu, Joy of Man's Desiring**. The lights come up to reveal a hilltop near Stanbrook Abbey at 11.50am on a bright sunny day.*

A Nun in her 50's is sitting on a mound of dirt. She smiles with great satisfaction as she drinks from a thermos. To look at her you'd never guess that she is in charge of a convent. Her veil is pinned back and she is wearing sun-glasses.

13

There is an oblong hole dug beside her. There are grave stones all around. From time to time dirt flies out of the hole, its spray narrowly missing the Nun whose name is Mother Raphael - the Mother Abbess at Stanbrook Abbey.

SISTER MIRIAM: (*from below, in the grave*) It should be ready by tomorrow.

MOTHER RAPHAEL: (*studying the grave*) Are you sure you're going to fit?

SISTER MIRIAM: I'll have room to wriggle my toes.

MOTHER RAPHAEL: Most people think it's morbid till they actually try it out. There's nothing like spending a day in your grave to get a healthy perspective on life. And don't dwell too much on Death when you're down there. Think about the days ahead - and how best you can use your time.

Sister Miriam, meanwhile, climbs out of her grave.

SISTER MIRIAM: (*panting with effort*) Yes, Mother.

MOTHER RAPHAEL: And be sure to bring a bucket. You'll get quite dizzy. Some Sisters throw up.

SISTER MIRIAM: Dizzy? Down here?

MOTHER RAPHAEL: Oh yes. When you're lying there watching the clouds roll by, you'll feel like you're spinning - and very fast too. (*confidentially, as she pours tea from the thermos for Miriam*) And if you listen hard enough, you can actually hear the world turn...So what did you find out about this thirty-four pounds?

14

SISTER MIRIAM: I went through our old Account Books. Two years ago we received by post an anonymous donation. For thirty-four pounds cash. The card that came with it said *Pray for Us.*

MOTHER RAPHAEL: *Us?*

SISTER MIRIAM: Should we give him a refund?

MOTHER RAPHAEL: What do *you* think? A man sends us money and asks for our prayers. Then two years later he turns up here drunk and smelly. Doesn't sound like we've managed to help him much at all. I don't blame him for feeling short-changed. (*almost sternly*) Now is there something else we should discuss before the Silence begins?

SISTER MIRIAM: No, Mother.

MOTHER RAPHAEL: Really? I noticed - at breakfast - that your eyes were very red.

SISTER MIRIAM: (*lying*) Conjunctivitis, Mother.

MOTHER RAPHAEL: You've not been crying?

Sister Miriam looks away awkwardly.

MOTHER RAPHAEL: At 20, nun's weep because they're homesick; at 40 because they're childless and at my age because they doubt God's existence and wonder if it's all been for nothing. But you, Sister Miriam, fit none of these categories. (*looking at her calmly but with disarming frankness*)

MOTHER RAPHAEL: I'm sorry you have a problem so great that you cannot confide it in me. It means I have failed you. After Chapel I'd like you to see your Confessor. Perhaps he can help.

SISTER MIRIAM: Mother - I -

Before Mother Raphael can reply, a distant bell begins to ring and the Six Hour Silence begins. No more conversation is allowed.

And Mother Raphael indicates, through sign language, that they must return to the Abbey.

SCENE THREE

The chapel at Stanbrook Abbey. Vespers are about to commence.

*Mother Raphael enters. She stands on stage holding a large, lighted candle. Sister Miriam and another young Nun, Sister Walburga, follow. They, too, are holding lighted candles. They are singing **Pie Jesu** (by Andrew Lloyd Webber).*

Sister Miriam moves away from the two other nuns and kneels in the Confessional.

On the other side of the Confessional - virtually unseen except in silhouette, is the Priest.

We must only see his vague outline.

Convent confessions can be brutal - and this one's no exception. Sister Miriam is very nervous and struggles to hide it.

16

PRIEST: (*forcefully*) So, Sister Miriam - why were you crying?

SISTER MIRIAM: I had a visitor. A drunken, brash American.

PRIEST: A man?

SISTER MIRIAM: (*uneasy*) Yes. A man.

PRIEST: Did you know him?

SISTER MIRIAM: I've never spoken to him before. And hope not to again.

PRIEST: Then why did he make you cry?

SISTER MIRIAM: (*with great reluctance*) His voice, Father. His voice - and his accent.

PRIEST: Such a fragile world you must live in if the voice of a drunk can upset it.

SISTER MIRIAM: He reminded me of someone - from my life before the convent.

PRIEST: A man?

SISTER MIRIAM: (*whispers*) Yes.

PRIEST: (*firmly*) I can't hear you.

SISTER MIRIAM: Yes. A man.

PRIEST: (*wearily*) It always comes down to this, doesn't it? You've been a nun for thirteen years but sex still rears its ugly head. Why didn't you tell this to the Mother Superior? Why did you feel the need to lie?

PRIEST: (*no reply*) Sister Miriam?

SISTER MIRIAM: She's a very fine woman - but she's not very worldly. And -

An awkward pause -

PRIEST: (*sternly*) And?

SISTER MIRIAM: (*with great effort and reluctance*) And I don't trust her with my memories.

PRIEST: (*sighs, almost bored*) What penance does a lie deserve? In the good old days you'd have flogged yourself - and felt much better for it. But since Vatican 2 we have to be subtle. (*suddenly inspired*) I know! I instruct you to talk to the Mother Abbess about all these memories that trouble you so much.

SISTER MIRIAM: (*horrified, tries to change his mind*) But we're not allowed to talk about the past.

PRIEST: Then I give you permission to do so. After all, Sister Miriam, this is not the Foreign Legion.

SISTER MIRIAM: (*alarmed*) Father - please -

PRIEST: You must learn to trust your superiors. (*allowing no further discussion he begins absolution*) Te ab solvo in nomine Patrii et Filii et Spiriti Sacti. Amen.

*Sister Miriam rises and the Nuns leave the stage, singing **The Flower Duet** by Delibes, in gentle harmony.*

SCENE FOUR

As the lights come up we can see Sister Miriam lying in her grave, contemplating Death. She remains visible throughout the scene.

Behind her, in the Visitors' Room at Stanbrook Abbey, Tyrone has returned to see the nuns. He is sitting, drinking, on one side of the grille.

On the other side of the grille we can see Mother Raphael. She sits facing the audience so that she is sideways to the grille. She has a cheque book on her lap and she is holding a pen.

MOTHER RAPHAEL: Here's the refund then. Thirty-four pounds. For your unanswered prayers. I'm sorry we disappointed you.

No reply from Tyrone. Just a belch.

MOTHER RAPHAEL: (*unfazed*) Now what name shall I write on the cheque?

TYRONE: (*very drunk*) Write - "Pay the Bearer Cash." Understand?

MOTHER RAPHAEL: (*says aloud as she writes*) Pay the Bearer Cash...

TYRONE: (*accusingly*) You're not Irish.

19

MOTHER RAPHAEL: No. I'm from London.

TYRONE: Where's the Irish one?

MOTHER RAPHAEL: In our cemetery.

TYRONE: She didn't sound sick to me.

MOTHER RAPHAEL: Every nun in our Order must dig her own grave - and lie in it - for a day - to prepare herself for death.

TYRONE: What if she wants to be buried somewhere else?

MOTHER RAPHAEL: We take a vow of Stability here. It means we can never leave Stanbrook.

TYRONE: So you're telling me that if she gets drunk - falls down and splits her skull - you won't let her out for an X-Ray?

MOTHER RAPHAEL: We get permission from our Bishop first.

TYRONE: (*with a drunk's obsession*) And what if you can't find him? What if he's gone to Brighton with a little piece of ass?

MOTHER RAPHAEL: Then either the nun recovers - or her grave is ready and waiting.

TYRONE: That doesn't sound very stable to me. (*disgusted*) Christ - you don't know - you don't know about Death. If you *did*, you wouldn't play games with it.

MOTHER RAPHAEL: (*interested, not sympathetic*) And what do *you* know? Can I ask? Is that why we were praying for you?

No reply. Instead Mother Raphael hears Tyrone get up - and lurch towards the door.

MOTHER RAPHAEL: (*calmly calling out*) Excuse me - you forgot your cheque.

And Mother Raphael slides the cheque through the little Offerings Drawer.

As Tyrone bends down to retrieve it, she can obviously smell his boozy breath.

MOTHER RAPHAEL: (*concerned*) Where will you go when you leave here?

TYRONE: (*being honest, not offensive*) Well I'm already drunk - so I might as well get laid. Don't suppose you know a whorehouse that will cash a convent's cheque?

MOTHER RAPHAEL: (*not shocked in the least*) Try *the Blue Garter* - in Soho. They send us a donation every year. (*calling after him*) Just don't expect a discount when you mention my name.

And we hear the door open as Tyrone stomps off.

And Mother Raphael blesses him - desperately - through the grille.

Tyrone - of course - does not see this. He would be furious if he did.

21

*On the sound-track we hear Eartha Kitt singing her wickedly funny hit **I Want to be Evil**.*

SCENE FIVE

Sister Miriam lies in her newly dug grave, eyes closed, arms folded across her chest. Mother Raphael is sitting on the ground above her, peeling an orange.

SISTER MIRIAM: (*almost nervously*) It feels a bit strange - being idle all day.

MOTHER RAPHAEL: It's to remind you, Sister Miriam, how thorough Death is. How it robs us of everything - who we are - what we do - nothing matters in the grave. So enjoy Life while you can. (*leaning over the grave in which Sister Miriam is lying*) I've brought you some lunch. Here!

And Mother Raphael drops an orange into the grave. She has a bag of them with her.

SISTER MIRIAM: (*politely*) No thank you.

And the orange comes rolling back out of the grave.

Mother Raphael shrugs - and begins to peel it for herself.

MOTHER RAPHAEL: (*sitting near the grave*) So what did your Confessor say? Did he give you the Foreign Legion speech?

SISTER MIRIAM: Yes. (*as an after-thought*) Oh - and he feels a good whipping might help.

MOTHER RAPHAEL: (*smiling fondly*) A whipping! Gosh, doesn't *that* take me back. In *my* day we really did it - flogged ourselves - and quite hard too. (*bites into orange and pulls a face*) Wish you'd change your mind about the orange. Sister Anselma gets offended if we don't eat everything in her orchard. Here. I *order* you to have one. (*tosses the orange into the grave*) Catch!

SISTER MIRIAM: Ouch!!

MOTHER RAPHAEL: Sorry.

SISTER MIRIAM: That hurt.

MOTHER RAPHAEL: Offer it up. (*casually*) You know I've never actually asked you why you came to this convent.

And now we see Sister Miriam lying in her grave. She sits up, reluctantly.

SISTER MIRIAM: Must I do this?

MOTHER RAPHAEL: Eat the orange?

SISTER MIRIAM: Answer questions.

MOTHER RAPHAEL: (*calmly peering into the grave*) You cry at night. You're deathly pale. You never ever laugh. I'd say you're clinically depressed. So yes. You must. Now - tell me all about him.

SISTER MIRIAM: (*a little alarmed at the Abbess's perspicacity*) Him?

MOTHER RAPHAEL: Usually when a nun's so coy, it means there's a man involved. Well - was he a tinker - tailor - soldier -

SISTER MIRIAM: Poet. (*covering her face with her hands*) He was a poet.

MOTHER RAPHAEL: (*slightly irritated*) Stop romanticising.

SISTER MIRIAM: He was.

And Sister Miriam tosses the orange back up at Mother Raphael.

MOTHER RAPHAEL: Ow.

SISTER MIRIAM: Sorry.

MOTHER RAPHAEL: Liar....Was he famous?

SISTER MIRIAM: He should have been.

Mother Raphael, meanwhile, begins to clean a nearby grave. Perhaps she starts to bury the oranges there.

MOTHER RAPHAEL: Recite something for me then. Something of his.

SISTER MIRIAM: (*alarmed at the prospect*) I forget.

Sister Miriam climbs from her grave, as if trying to escape from the questions.

MOTHER RAPHAEL: Then you can't have loved him very much.

SISTER MIRIAM: (*stung, begins to recite*) *Seeing the sky placid, in spite of soot and heartache, I am reminded to pray. Redemption, like our janitor, comes as we go home, a stooped man turning out the lights.*

MOTHER RAPHAEL: Oh. I *like* that.

SISTER MIRIAM: I didn't. Not at first. I always thought Redemption should switch *on* the lights.

MOTHER RAPHAEL: How did you meet him?

SISTER MIRIAM: (*distressed*) Please, Mother, I can't...

MOTHER RAPHAEL: (*firmly*) How did you meet him, Sister Miriam?

SISTER MIRIAM: (*reluctantly*) He met me. He rang me - in my hotel room - after he'd heard me on the radio.

MOTHER RAPHAEL: (*surprised*) *You?* On the wireless.

SISTER MIRIAM: I just sang a few songs sometimes.

MOTHER RAPHAEL: (*smiles and starts weeding the grave*) And what was this poet's name?

SISTER MIRIAM: (*with real torment*) Is there nothing I can do to make you stop?

MOTHER RAPHAEL: It's pretty hard to bribe someone who's taken a vow of poverty. (*gently but with some determination*) Tell me his name please, Sister Miriam.

A pause.

SISTER MIRIAM: *(trying not to cry as she says the name for the first time in years)* Richard.

Suddenly, on a different part of the stage, the lights reveal a very handsome young man nervously hovering over a telephone as he says - simultaneously -

RICHARD: *(nervously into the telephone)* Richard. My name is Richard. Richard Selig. And I'm downstairs in the foyer.

Young Mary O'Hara is on the other end of the telephone. She is dressed in a beautiful gown. Her harp can be seen nearby.

YOUNG MARY: *(brusquely into the telephone)* And what exactly do you want Richard Selig?

RICHARD: To invite you to dinner of course.

YOUNG MARY: I don't have time for jokes. I'm about to go On Air. Goodbye.

RICHARD: Oh please Miss O'Hara. Don't hang up. I paid the desk clerk two pounds ten to call you to the phone. I heard the show you did last night and - well I knew then and there I just *had* to meet you. Do you believe in Fate?

YOUNG MARY: I believe that it's rude to ring someone in the middle of a radio broadcast.

RICHARD: Well - since I've offended you, let me apologise - by taking you out for coffee.

A male voice calls out -

RADIO STATION EMPLOYEE: (Voice Only) On Air in two minutes, Miss O'Hara!

YOUNG MARY: I hate to disappoint you, Richard, but you've "done" your two pounds ten. I can't *stand* Americans.

RICHARD: (*not the least bit offended - in fact he's interested*) Yeah? Why's that?

YOUNG MARY: They're vulgar, brash and pushy. No self-respecting gentleman would telephone a stranger to whom he hasn't been introduced.

RICHARD: What do you think I'm doing now? And not a bad job, either... (*persuasively*) Listen - do you want to go back to your hotel *alone* when you should be out dancing on this perfect spring evening?

YOUNG MARY: Oh - I never dance.

RICHARD: Why not?

YOUNG MARY: Because I'm six feet tall - and pigeon toed. So it's not a pretty sight.

This is - of course - a lie.

YOUNG MARY: Now if you don't mind -

RICHARD: But they said in the paper that you used to be a model.

YOUNG MARY: (*caught out - but thinking quick*) That's right. I did the before photos - in some ads for tinea cream. My feet are deformed, you see.

RICHARD: This is *amazing* - absolutely amazing. My toes are completely webbed - like a duck's. (*brightly*) And I have a hunchback too! We've known each other a mere thirty seconds and already we have so much in common! Now when can I meet you?

YOUNG MARY: Meet me?

RICHARD: Yes. You can show me round London if you like. I'm a student here. Did I mention that? And not *just* a student. I'm a Rhodes scholar.

YOUNG MARY: Well aren't *you* the confident one? As a matter of fact, I *have* a boyfriend. Several - to be brutally honest.

RICHARD: No you don't. There's no one in your life. There *can't* be. You see...you and I are *meant* for each other.

YOUNG MARY: Do you do this often? Throw yourself at total strangers?

RICHARD: You're not a stranger. Not to *me*. When you sing, you bare your soul completely. You were practically naked on my radio tonight.

YOUNG MARY: (*annoyed*) Mind your mouth now, Mr Selig.

RICHARD: Mr Selig! What happened to "Richard"?

YOUNG MARY: He got a mite too forward.

Richard realises he is making a bad impression. So he says - desperately -

RICHARD: Please - please - give me a chance. (with unexpected intensity) I know you're famous - and I'm just a student - but no sound I've ever heard has made me feel the way your voice does. (almost desperately) There's a cafe on Delaney Road. I'll be there tomorrow at noon.

YOUNG MARY: Do you really think I'll go out with you? Why I don't even know what you look like.

RICHARD: (*eagerly*) I look just like - (*modesty almost forbids*) - Laurence Olivier -

YOUNG MARY: You said you had a hunchback -

RICHARD: - in Richard the Third.

Mary laughs. And, in spite of herself, she's about to say "Yes" when -

RADIO STATION EMPLOYEE: (Voice Only) One minute - Miss O'Hara - and the producer's getting anxious!

YOUNG MARY: (*to Richard*) I'm sorry. Really. But this wouldn't work.

RICHARD: Please.

YOUNG MARY: I'll leave two pounds ten at the reception desk. You can get it when I've gone. (*firmly*) Don't go wasting your money on phone calls to strangers. There's no such thing as "meant for each other".

RICHARD: Wait - wait -

YOUNG MARY: Goodbye.

And Mary hangs up. She walks over to the harp, and sits down.

RADIO ANNOUNCER: (Voice Only) And now on BBC 1 - Miss Mary O'Hara.

*And Mary begins to sing **Blow the Wind Southerly**, a song of desperate and unfulfilled love.*

As she sings, we can see Richard Selig, listening with longing to the radio.

And as the song continues, Sister Miriam becomes so caught up in her memory that she joins in, unaware that she is doing so. Soon both Young Mary and Sister Miriam are singing the song together. Then Young Mary's voice fades, and Sister Miriam finishes it...

Then Sister Miriam - says from the grave -

SISTER MIRIAM: But in spite of myself I went there - to that Cafe on Delaney Road.

MOTHER RAPHAEL: Why? Why did you go?

SISTER MIRIAM: His voice. There was something in it that - that puzzled me - that seemed to be saying *more* than just "I want to take you out"... It's different when you can't see someone. You listen more to their sounds than the words they say.

SISTER MIRIAM: (*sadly*) I heard another voice like his - only very recently.

And the lights come up on Tyrone. He is pressing himself
  anxiously against a door as several (unseen) men try very
  hard to force it open.

TYRONE: Help! Help! Goddamn those nuns!!!

*Darkness... On the soundtrack we hear Eartha Kitt singing **I'm***
  Just an Old Fashioned Girl.

SCENE SIX

Sister Miriam is on her knees, scrubbing the floor. As she scrubs,
  she has been absent-mindedly singing a song from her past
  *- the last few verses of **Old Fashioned Girl**. She is so busy*
  concentrating on her cleaning that she does not even
  realise she is singing it.

Tyrone, meanwhile, has entered the Visitor's Area. Tyrone
  listens for a few seconds, fascinated as Sister Miriam sings
  "I'm just a pilgrim at heart, oh so pure and genteel, catch
  me in Las Vegas when I'm at the spinning wheel!".

Then Tyrone rings the bell.

SISTER MIRIAM: Who's there?

TYRONE: Lovely hymn.

SISTER MIRIAM: (*embarrassed*) Oh - it's you.

TYRONE: One of my favourites.

SISTER MIRIAM: I trust you're well.

TYRONE: To be honest I am not. I had a bit of trouble this morning.

SISTER MIRIAM: (*judgmental*) No doubt you were intoxicated.

TYRONE: Fortunately yes. Otherwise I might have broken some bones. But drunks - like kittens - always land on their feet. (*sits down very carefully*) I went to this hotel in Soho, stayed all night, even paid in advance with a thirty-four pound cheque from Stanbrook Abbey. Are you listening?

SISTER MIRIAM: (*vaguely*) Yes...Yes.

TYRONE: Now picture this: 10am this morning , the sun is shining, the mini-bar empty and I'm fast asleep where I passed-out on the floor. Suddenly the door to my room flies open and the biggest man I've ever seen, picks me up and dangles me out the window - holding on - and only *just* - to my ankles.

SISTER MIRIAM: I don't mean to preach but these things happen when you drink.

TYRONE: I asked him if we'd met before and what I'd done to annoy him. He said something about my cheque being rubber. My cheque from Stanbrook Abbey.

SISTER MIRIAM: (*looks up, alarmed*) (What?)

TYRONE: There's nothing in the convent's account. Zilch! Zero! Goose-Egg! You see money's not like the loaves and the fishes. You aren't guaranteed an endless supply.

SISTER MIRIAM: (*alarmed and embarrassed*) Oh dear. Oh dear. I don't know what to say. Did he hurt you?

TYRONE: Not much. Lucky for me I was on the ground floor. But I've got one week to pay - and then they'll send their hit men after me.

SISTER MIRIAM: You better go to the police.

TYRONE: They *are* the police. So I'm going to need the cash. Right now.

SISTER MIRIAM: We don't have 34 pounds in cash. (*gets an idea*) Wait on. There's a money box next to the rack out there. When visitors buy our handicrafts we ask them to donate.

TYRONE: (*picking up box*) Where's the key?

SISTER MIRIAM: Oh it isn't locked. If anyone wants *our* money, they must be pretty desperate - why make things harder for them?

Tyrone, meanwhile, takes some coins out of the box.

TYRONE: (*disappointed*) Half a crown. Half a lousy crown.

But Tyrone pockets it anyway. Then he notices some hand-made cards at the bottom of the wire rack, just below the doilies.

TYRONE: (*with grudging admiration*) Hey - these aren't bad.

SISTER MIRIAM: The doilies?

TYRONE: Nah. They're trash. One sneeze and they'll fall apart. (*holding a card up*) There are cards here. With leaves. Real leaves by the looks of it. On deckle-edged paper. Very, very nice. (*almost accusingly*) Too nice for *this* place. Where did *these* come from?

SISTER MIRIAM: (*with great reluctance*) I made them.

TYRONE: You're joking. *You*? How much do you flog them for?

SISTER MIRIAM: A shilling.

TYRONE: I could sell these at the flea-markets. (*thinking aloud*) Hand-made and artsy-fartsy ...Mmm...Ten shillings each. (*to Sister Miriam*) I'll need sixty-eight by Thursday.

SISTER MIRIAM: I can't make sixty-eight leaf-cards in a week!

TYRONE: Why not? It's autumn. I'll lend you a rake... (*thinking, genuinely enthusiastic*) Tell you what - I'm a reasonable man - write something on them - in that fancy church scrawl -

SISTER MIRIAM: Calligraphy?

TYRONE: Yeah. And I'll sell 'em for a quid. So I'll just need thirty four. And I want a card for *me*. I want *Danny Boy*. The entire song. I like to sing it when I've had a few - but I can never remember the words. (*not joking, and almost tactfully*) You *can* write, can't you? I mean it's nothing to be ashamed of. I know how poor the Irish are and -

SISTER MIRIAM: (*furious*) I'm probably breaking most of my vows - and earning myself a few centuries in Purgatory - but right now it's worth it. (*loudly*) Go away!

Tyrone re-acts with an unexpected ferocity - almost desperation.

TYRONE: Believe me, lady, I'd love to. If you like I'll send the hit-men here. It was your cheque.

SISTER MIRIAM: That's blackmail.

But Sister Miriam starts to relent.

SISTER MIRIAM: (*firmly, grimly*) Look - I'll do psalms and proverbs and minor prayers. Not sentimental piffle.

TYRONE: (*pleased and having a swig of whiskey*) I've really upset you, haven't I?

SISTER MIRIAM: Upset? No nun has ever yelled at a guest in the four hundred years this Abbey's been here. Imagine the penance I'll get when I confess!

TYRONE: What do you look like?

SISTER MIRIAM: What?

TYRONE: Well it's hard to fight with someone if you don't know what they look like. Describe yourself.

SISTER MIRIAM: I...don't know.

TYRONE: Come on. You're being coy!

SISTER MIRIAM: I haven't seen my face for over ten years. We don't have mirrors here.

TYRONE: (*astonished*) Not at all? That's barbaric.

SISTER MIRIAM: It's actually very liberating. You can go grey - put on weight - get pimples - and never ever know. (*touching her face*) By now - I suppose - I'm stooped and wrinkled.

TYRONE: (*perceptively*) Don't you *miss* yourself, Sister? Miss your face? Miss perfume? Miss admiring whistles?

Before Sister Miriam can reply, a bell rings a few times, then stops.

SISTER MIRIAM: I have to go. I'm reading the Lesson. And it's a very big feast day.

TYRONE: (*not really interested*) Yeah? Who's the lucky saint?

SISTER MIRIAM: (*eagerly*) Saint Walburga of Buckfast.

TYRONE: (*laughs*) With a name like *that*, she had to be a virgin. Well - was she?

No reply. Just annoyed silence.

TYRONE: Sister - I asked you a religious question.

SISTER MIRIAM: (*reluctantly*) She cut her nose off with a knife so the Vikings wouldn't rape her.

TYRONE: (*laughs*) No wonder they don't have mirrors in convents!

And Sister Miriam slams the grille door shut. Tyrone's done it again.

SCENE SEVEN

A voice from the darkness calls out -

RICHARD: Mary? Mary?

The lights come up to reveal Richard Selig standing outside a door.

RICHARD: You can't hide in that toilet all day. You'll have to come out eventually. You don't like me very much, do you?

YOUNG MARY: (*primly, as she emerges*) To be honest, I do not.

RICHARD: (*not the least bit worried*) Is it my accent?

YOUNG MARY: No.

RICHARD: My jokes?

YOUNG MARY: No.

RICHARD: Well it can't be my clothes. This shirt cost a fortune.

YOUNG MARY: I didn't think you'd be so good looking. It's not *healthy* in a man.

And Richard laughs.

YOUNG MARY: I'm serious. *"The handsome are the first to sin."* The Sisters taught us that.

RICHARD: (*amused*) Really? And what else did the Sisters teach you?

YOUNG MARY: That girls who pursued attractive males would lose their bloom and end up like Sucked Oranges.

Richard casually removes an orange from his jacket and begins to peel it.

RICHARD: Can I go out with you again?

YOUNG MARY: (*shakes her head*) Go bald - or put on weight. And then I'll reconsider.

RICHARD: (*peeved*) All right. Have it your way. I can get any dame I want.. (*earnestly, desperately*) The trouble is - I want *you*. When I heard you on the wireless you wrecked poetry forever. You killed Keats and Shelley - and even T.S. Eliot. (*with real passion*) Because you made me see that words are nothing - just shells to hold sounds. (*embarrassed but sincere*) And every sound your voice creates has a - a taste and a colour that my whole body longs for.

Young Mary hesitates, then turns and looks at Richard - and her destiny.

RICHARD: Let me see you one more time. Please.

YOUNG MARY: Perhaps.

They are standing very, very close to each other now.

RICHARD: Am I allowed to kiss you then - to sort of - seal the deal?

YOUNG MARY: (*tempted*) No. The Sisters said no kissing. At least for the first three dates.

RICHARD: I see...So when do the Sisters say that...I can tell you that I love you?

YOUNG MARY: (*not annoyed in the slightest*) You are the forward type, aren't you?

And Young Mary looks at Richard. They move closer together. And in spite of the nuns, they embrace.

RICHARD: (*still holding her*) Now that we've kissed - and know each other better - (*hesitant for once*) -- there's something I have to warn you about.

YOUNG MARY: Warn me? (*getting worried*) You're not rich - are you?

RICHARD: (*surprised*) That's a *fault*?

YOUNG MARY: (*not joking*) It certainly *is*. A good-looking man with dollars in his pocket - you'd attract other women like raw meat gathers sharks. And I do not intend to go through life as the *first* Mrs Richard Selig.

RICHARD: You think I want to *marry* you?

YOUNG MARY: (*caught off-guard*) I'm being theoretical.

Richard stands in front of Young Mary - and is suddenly quite serious.

RICHARD: (*gravely*) What I have to say is *worse* - far worse than being rich. (*with urgency*) Don't leave me after I tell you. Please.

Richard hesitates then tries to take Mary's hand - but she pulls it away.

YOUNG MARY: (*angry*) You have a wife - don't you? Back in New York. Oh the Sisters were right about you Protestants! I should never have -

RICHARD: (*quickly interrupting*) I have a lump!

A pause. Young Mary looks at him - not understanding.

RICHARD: (*calmly this time*) I have a lump.

YOUNG MARY: (*laughs with relief*) A lump?

RICHARD: (*nods, smiles gently*) It's a good thing in a way. Because it heightens all your senses - and lets you see what really matters. Things you might have taken *years* to learn - you suddenly understand. And because of that - you have more courage. Courage to phone up famous singers and ask them out on dates.

YOUNG MARY: (*relieved*) A lump doesn't matter. I don't care about *looks*.

RICHARD: (*calmly*) It's not about my looks.

YOUNG MARY: (*hesitates then laughs*) Don't try and tell me you're *dying*, Richard. Talk about neurotic poets. A stronger, fitter man I've never-

Richard takes Mary's hand - not roughly - but suddenly - and presses it against his upper groin.

He holds her hand there as he says -

RICHARD: It's called Hodgkin's Disease. It likes healthy, young males. It's a form of cancer and it often kills. There. Now you know.

And Richard releases Mary's hand.

YOUNG MARY: How long has that been there?

RICHARD: Two months. My surgeon's very hopeful. He said - if I want - I could read *War & Peace* and live long enough to finish it.

YOUNG MARY: (*whispers*) Oh Richard...

RICHARD: (*calmly but with urgency*) I'm telling you all this because I do things very quickly now. And in my heart - and in my head - I imagine us married already. You're the *first* Mrs Richard Selig. And we're just back from our honeymoon. But the glamour's worn off a bit I'm afraid. You've discovered I snore and I've found out that you can't cook.

YOUNG MARY: (*upset*) Don't joke about this, Richard -.

RICHARD: (*continues talking in the same tone*) But we love each other more than anything. And cancer or not - my whole body hums like those crickets that sing with the joy of summer.

YOUNG MARY: (*close to tears*) This can't be happening - not to *you*. There must be something we can do.

RICHARD: Maybe there is. What's your middle name?

Mary looks at him, puzzled.

YOUNG MARY: Therese. Why?

Richard kneels - and Mary kneels with him, wondering what on earth is going on.

RICHARD: (*tenderly as he holds her*) Will *you* - Mary Therese O'Hara - take *me* - Richard Marvin Sclig - to have and to hold - in sickness and in dubious health - for richer or poorer - though mostly "poorer" since poets don't make money -

Mary is now looking at Richard. They are kneeling together and he is holding her hand as if about to slip a ring onto it.

RICHARD: - but with all the love a man can bring to the woman he needs and adores - forever and ever - disregarding Death entirely - because it cannot and will not end our love?

A pause. Mary looks at Richard - overcome by emotion - loving him.

RICHARD: (*smiles*) If you don't say "Yes" I'll feel pretty foolish, Mary.

But Mary cannot speak. She tries but the words won't come. Instead she nods. And then Mary and Richard Selig, still on their knees, hug each other desperately.

On the soundtrack we hear the sounds of wedding bells. And on the screen we see the following headline: "Mary O'Hara Marries Non-Catholic!"

SCENE EIGHT

The stage lights reveal Sister Miriam sitting near the grille, peeling potatoes over a large steel bowl lined with newspaper. Mother Raphael stands nearby.

MOTHER RAPHAEL: Are you happy here - at Stanbrook?

SISTER MIRIAM: (*calmly*) I was content - until the American came. He's not a *bit* like Richard. Yet he *is*. Same voice - same accent - confidence - cheekiness.

SISTER MIRIAM: (*not angrily but honestly*) There are things about Richard I can't bear to remember - not even now - after all these years. But this man has brought them back. I wish he'd find somewhere else to go.

MOTHER RAPHAEL: Or someone else to talk to?

SISTER MIRIAM: (*hopefully*) Yes.

MOTHER RAPHAEL: You're not the first nun to be troubled by her past. This is what I tell the others - the widows like yourself. Even in Death you're still married to your husband. So do not resist your memories of him. You must let them run their course. It will be good for you - I think - to keep speaking to this American.

SISTER MIRIAM: (*interrupting to object*) No -

43

MOTHER RAPHAEL: (*raising her hand, refusing to listen, then calmly peeling away*) All of us - at some stage here - must imitate poor Saint Walburga. We must take a knife and hack away at a part of our lives we cherish. Sometimes it's all for nothing - and the Vikings rape us anyway. And sometimes - if we're lucky - through the gristle and the blood, we glimpse the Divine.

The bell rings several times, stridently.

TYRONE: Hello? Anyone home? (*ringing the Visitors' Bell*) Avon calling!!

Mother Raphael stands up. Sister Miriam looks at her pleadingly. She doesn't want to talk to Tyrone.

But Mother Raphael is unmoved. She makes a gesture towards the Visitors' Grille, indicating "He's all yours" to Sister Miriam.

SISTER MIRIAM: I'm here.

TYRONE: You took your time. What's that smell?

SISTER MIRIAM: Our potatoes. I'm peeling them for dinner.

TYRONE: You Irish and your spuds!

Sister Miriam suddenly hurls a potato at the grille - right where she thinks Tyrone is standing.

Tyrone jumps in fright.

TYRONE: Jesus Christ!

The potato bounces off the grille and lands near Sister Miriam.

SISTER MIRIAM: Sorry. One of them slipped.

TYRONE: That spud needs an exorcism. Here - drop it in the tray. *I* better do it.

SISTER MIRIAM: Oh no. I'm not supposed to -

TYRONE: (*with unexpected charm*) Go on. Put your feet up. We've got business to discuss.

So Sister Miriam puts the potato and the peeler in the little drawer that connects the Visitors with the Nuns.

Tyrone sits down on the other side of the grille, opens the drawer, removes the potato and looks at it.

TYRONE: You call *this* a potato?

SISTER MIRIAM: We didn't have a very good crop this year.

TYRONE: I'll say. It looks like a plum with the mumps. (*as he begins to peel the potato*) I take it you're doing this for penance.

SISTER MIRIAM: Hardly. Peeling the potatoes is the most coveted job in the convent.

TYRONE: Yeah? Why?

SISTER MIRIAM: Because the scraps must be wrapped in newspaper. And as we don't normally get the papers, the lucky nun has a chance to read.

TYRONE: (*surprised*) You're not allowed *newspapers*!

SISTER MIRIAM: Oh sometimes we get *The Catholic Weekly* - after the Bishop has censored it. So what's this business we need to discuss?

TYRONE: First of all - are the leaf-cards done?

SISTER MIRIAM: Of course. All thirty-four.

TYRONE: Good. I'll sell them at the markets - and we'll split the profits fifty-fifty.

SISTER MIRIAM: Oh, no. That's not right.

TYRONE: (*defensive*) But *I'm* the one doing the leg work.

SISTER MIRIAM: Exactly. So *you* must keep it all.

TYRONE: (*frustrated*) You nuns! (*calmly but exasperated*) I am trying to rip you off, Sister. And you're supposed to stop me. When *I* say "Fifty-fifty", *You* say "Go to hell! Sixty-forty." And we barter it from there. That's how the world of finance works.

SISTER MIRIAM: But I've taken a vow of poverty. I'm not allowed to make *any* money - sixty-forty or otherwise. (*reaches down for a packet on the floor*) Here are some of your leaf-cards by the way.

And Sister Miriam passes the leaf cards to Tyrone, through the grille drawer.

Tyrone picks up the leaf cards. He is caught off-guard by their simplicity and their beauty.

46

TYRONE: (*mutters*) Wow...Your talent's as big as your temper....Oh the hippies'll *snap* these up. (*holding leaf card up to the light*) Just *looking* at this could send you on a "trip".

SISTER MIRIAM: I didn't understand a single word you said.

TYRONE: You'll bring comfort and joy to a lot of young people.

Tyrone takes a swig of whiskey and Sister Miriam becomes a bit curious about him.

SISTER MIRIAM: (*gently*) What did you do - in your life - *before* alcohol?

TYRONE: (*firmly*) If you want to be a successful drunk you don't talk about the past.

SISTER MIRIAM: But *something* must have made you like this.

TYRONE: (*rising, threatened*) I've got to go.

SISTER MIRIAM: Please. I'd - like to know. (*has an idea*) Yes. That's my payment. I'm bartering - just like you suggested. If you want the rest of the cards, you must tell me. Otherwise I'll tear them up.

TYRONE: That's a rotten thing to do after *I* peeled your potatoes.

SISTER MIRIAM: And since we're going to be business partners, I'll need to know your name.

TYRONE: Rumplestiltskin. It's Jewish. What's yours?

SISTER MIRIAM: Miriam. Mine's Hebrew too. For "Mary". (*pauses briefly, then*) Are you married, Mr Stiltskin?

TYRONE: (*angrily*) Hey! Some things you don't make jokes about!

SISTER MIRIAM: Oh - I'm sorry.

TYRONE: (*hesitates*) I had a wife. Her name was - (*cannot bring himself to say it*) - she once made me send money - to Stanbrook Abbey.

SISTER MIRIAM: (*gently*) Why?

Tyrone takes another swig of whiskey.

TYRONE: (*with great difficulty*) She believed in prayers and miracles.

SISTER MIRIAM: (*with tact*) And what were we praying for exactly? Was she ill?

TYRONE: (*getting upset*) What's it to you, lady?

SISTER MIRIAM: I'm sorry. You must have loved her very much.

A pause. Tyrone grimaces as a painful memory shatters his alcoholic haze.

TYRONE: (*upset and threatened by the memory*) None of your goddamn business. Keep your stinking cards. I can't do this!

Tyrone heads for the door.

SISTER MIRIAM: (*desperately*) Wait. Please. (*searching for an excuse to get him back*) You've got my potato!

Tyrone hurls the potato at the grille.

SISTER MIRIAM: (*with urgency*) I can't let you leave like this. They gave us this leaflet - on How to Communicate. Most of our guests are just pious old ladies - or tourists who've missed the turn-off to London. But the leaflet says - and it's most emphatic - we must never let a guest leave in an upset state of mind. (*uneasily*) So why don't we chat for a couple of minutes.

TYRONE: Chat?

SISTER MIRIAM: Yes.

TYRONE: Are you worried that I'll *neck* myself? Take the dry dive - is that what you think? Well go on. *You're* the one who's read the leaflet. Chat!

Sister Miriam gazes around for something to talk about.

A pause. Sister Miriam looks desperately at the newspaper, searching for a topic of interest.

SISTER MIRIAM: Um... (*trying to make it sound interesting*) Doesn't Richard Nixon have a warm and kindly face?

TYRONE: It's not polite - discussing politics.

SISTER MIRIAM: Is he a politician? Oh. I'm sorry. (*sees something else - quite alarming*) Gosh. It says here "*Abba*

Fever is spreading over England." How strange. The bishop usually warns us when there's an epidemic coming. Do you know if there are shots for it?

But Tyrone does not reply. Instead he begins to laugh. It is almost a painful experience. Then he squats against the wall.

SISTER MIRIAM: (*gently*) Your wife - you said we were praying for her. Why?

TYRONE: (*hesitates, then*) The doctors said she'd never have children.

SISTER MIRIAM: And we failed her, did we?

TYRONE: We were on holidays in Ireland when we found out she was finally "knocked-up". We drove into Belfast. To celebrate. It was a Friday. Bright and warm. I dropped her outside a cafe then I went to buy some roses. She loved roses. I bought every one the florist had and rushed back to meet her. I was three blocks away when I heard the explosion. Then silence. Then screams. These terrible screams. I ran back so fast I was leaping over fences....But there wasn't much left of Jean or the cafe. The IRA did their job too well.
(*angrily*) Do you know what really gets to me? They say a bomb *smells* before it explodes. A stinking smell - like dog-shit. It's caused by the detonator melting down. But Jean would have thought she'd *stepped* in something. She would have been mortified. She would have died *embarrassed*. Silly isn't it? But that's what worries me. Not the injustice or the pain or the futility. Just the thought of my wife - all alone - cringing from shame - before those Irish bastards murdered her.

50

Darkness...On the soundtrack we hear nuns singing **Benedictine**
Chants*.*

SCENE NINE

Tyrone's "digs" in London. We only need to see the bed - a
smelly, filthy- sheeted mess.

Tyrone is sleeping off a "bender" when the telephone rings.
Tyrone reaches out and, without opening his eyes, lifts the
receiver and drops it again, hanging-up on the caller.
Tyrone resumes his sleeping.

But the phone rings once more. This time Tyrone answers it.

TYRONE: (*into receiver*) Piss off!

And Tyrone slams the phone down - and rolls over to sleep.

But the phone rings again. And this infuriates Tyrone. Dozing
drunks - like sleeping tigers - should never be disturbed.

TYRONE: (*annoyed*) You deaf or something. (*pause*) Eileen? I
don't know any Eileen. (*pause*) - from the pub? (*and now*
memories of the previous night come flooding back) Oh,
yes. (*with an inward groan*) Yes ,of course. I remember
you now. Comrade Eileen.

Tyrone sits on his bed. He takes a bottle of Scotch . He puts it
between his legs and tries to open it - as he talks on the
phone.

TYRONE: Hell, Eileen, what can I say? I don't normally drink
alcohol. But someone *persuaded* me to have a shandy -

51

which is why I threw up on that old cardigan of yours. (*pause*) Cashmere? Oh. So I guess you want me to pay for the cleaning. OK. OK. There's a cheque in the mail.

Tyrone is about to hang up - when he is asked another question.

TYRONE: What cards? (*pause*) The ones with the leaves stuck on them? Oh those. I must have dropped some when I - fainted on you. (*pause, impatiently*) No - *I* didn't make them. Someone from the Midlands did. (*reluctantly*) I happened to visit this - (*hesitates*) - place - and they were on display - on a rack.

A very thirsty Tyrone continues his struggle with the bottle.

TYRONE: Well the person who makes them can't travel to London - so I volunteered to sell them at the markets. (*impatiently*) Look - I have to go - I'm trying to open my breakfast. (*more impatiently*) Because they don't let anyone *out* from there. It's an institution, understand? We even have to talk through a grille. (*pause, shocked*) Dartmoor!? (*pause, sarcastic*) Yeah - I'm absolutely *thrilled* that you're so fond of Prison Art. Of course I'll tell him. (*pause, shocked*) You want to order one hundred cards?! *One hundred!* (*thinking fast*) Well I can't make any promises - he's in "solitary" right now. (*pause*) He threw a potato at one of the warders. They're a very strict Order - I mean jail.

Tyrone runs his hand through his hair and tries to sober up.

TYRONE: No - No - he's doing Life. The hard way, too. Their cells are *freezing*. And they don't have any mirrors. (*pause*) Well in case they *mutilate* themselves. Only last week an inmate sliced off his nose - (*pause*) - so he wouldn't get pack-raped of course!

And Tyrone takes a well-earned swig from the bottle, then -

TYRONE: Well - the cards are - *two* guineas each. (*trying to stay calm*) Yes...cash'll be fine. (*pause*) Honorary Artist for the Communist Party? He'll be so thrilled when I tell him. (*pause*) Eileen - please - you're making me blush. All I want is to help my fellow man.

Darkness.

SCENE TEN

*And we suddenly hear three voices sing brightly and joyfully - A-lleluia! A-lleluia! A-lleluia! Sister Miriam, Sister Walburga and Mother Raphael are singing the **Alleluia Chorus** from **Handel's Messiah**.*

Tyrone enters the stage carrying a large Hessian bag. He deposits it in front of the grille. Tyrone rings the Visitor's bell. He is obviously in a hurry.

Sister Miriam enters the Visitors' Area to answer the bell.

SISTER MIRIAM: Who's there?

TYRONE: It's me.

SISTER MIRIAM: Our visiting time is over.

TYRONE: Can't stay. Gotta dash. Thanks to you I've got a date.

SISTER MIRIAM: Thanks to *me*?

TYRONE: I need one hundred more leaf-cards pronto. They're a huge hit out here.

Outside a car horn blasts.

TYRONE: (*calls impatiently to the unseen car driver*) Hang on! (*to Sister Miriam*) There's a present for you in the foyer too. I know I'm supposed to leave donations in the drawer - but if you want to get this one, you're going to have to come outside.

Then Tyrone exits.

SISTER MIRIAM: What on earth are you up to now? (*no reply*) Hello? Hello?

And Sister Miriam undoes the connecting door impatiently.

SISTER MIRIAM: (*mumbling angrily*) If this is a trick to see my face - you'll also see the back of my hand!

But Sister Miriam stops. The Visitors' Area is empty. The only thing there is a large Hessian bag waiting for her. It smells terrible. Beside it is an envelope and a brown paper parcel.

SISTER MIRIAM: (*sniffs, pulls a face*) Oh...

Sister Miriam picks up the note and we hear Tyrone's voice reciting its contents.

TYRONE'S VOICE: "Happy Birthday. It's a nine pound bag of premium chicken manure. From what I've seen of your potatoes, they need all the help they can get. Please resist the temptation to roll round in it for penance. The envelope is from a guy called Jeremy Seagull - he's a hippy at the markets. He'd like you to make him some cards - using leaves from a plant called *cannabis*. (*innocently*) Since you don't have any growing here, he's sent you some seeds - to help you get started."

As she goes to pick up the seeds she notices an LP record in a large brown paper bag.

SISTER MIRIAM: (*reading the note*) "And in the paper bag you'll find the best Danny Boy I've ever heard. If *this* doesn't make you cry, stick your head in the chicken shit and leave it there! Take care of those potatoes. Nuns need their carbohydrates too."

Sister Miriam smiles. She opens the paper bag - and removes an L.P. Record. She looks at it - then drops to the floor - as surprisingly - as unexpectedly as possible.

As Sister Miriam lies, unconscious, we see the cover of the L.P. that she has just gazed at. The L.P. Cover says: **Mary O'Hara Sings Danny Boy & Other Favourites.**

And the black and white photograph on the L.P. cover shows Mary O'Hara - shortly before her marriage - arm in arm with Richard Selig, her soon-to-be-husband. They are smiling happily, full of warmth and love and joy.

This is the first time Sister Miriam has seen a photo of herself - or her husband - since she entered the convent 13 years earlier.

It is such a shocking reminder of all she has lost that you can't really blame her for fainting.

*As Sister Miriam lies unconscious on the floor, we hear Simon & Garfunkel on the soundtrack, singing the **Bookends** theme. "Preserve your memories. They're all that's left you..."*

The slide of the L.P. Cover remains on screen for the next scene as well.

SCENE ELEVEN

Sister Miriam is recovering from her faint. Mother Raphael stands nearby, clutching the LP.

Mother Raphael reads aloud from the record sleeve's notes. Sister Miriam hates this - but is powerless to object.

MOTHER RAPHAEL: (*reads*) "With her fourteen records all best-sellers, it goes without saying that Mary O'Hara is already an icon to Flower-Children everywhere." (*looks up, puzzled*) What could that mean - *Flower Children*? Would you like me to ask the gardener?

SISTER MIRIAM: (*politely*) No, Mother.

MOTHER RAPHAEL: Probably wise. Fred gets a bit confused these days. (*smiles at the memory*) Remember when he told us there were Americans on the moon!

SISTER MIRIAM: (*calmly, without emotion*) I apologise for fainting. I haven't seen my husband's photo - or mine - for over ten years. But I feel much better now. So please may I get up?

MOTHER RAPHAEL: All right. But don't kneel in Mass. And don't ever scare me like that again...

MOTHER RAPHAEL: (*as Sister Miriam rises*) So what shall I do with this gift of yours?

SISTER MIRIAM: (*indicates the fire*) I'd like you to dispose of it.

MOTHER RAPHAEL: (*surprised*) What?

SISTER MIRIAM: (*calmly*) Mary O'Hara is gone for good. She's as dead as the man beside her. Please let her rest in peace.

MOTHER RAPHAEL: You mean this poor piece of vinyl has journeyed all the way here just to end up in our furnace? Well - since it's causing you so much distress -

SISTER MIRIAM: (*suddenly, with regret*) Richard was the one - *he* should have been famous - not me. (*sadly*) I had no wish - no right - to outshine him. All my records re-released while he hardly even made it into print. (*hurt, not angry*) This is so *unjust* of God.

MOTHER RAPHAEL: God often seems unjust to us. And perhaps he is. (*looking at the LP sleeve*) How long since you've sung these songs?

SISTER MIRIAM: A dozen years. The week before I joined the convent. I did my final concert - and I vowed I'd never perform again.

MOTHER RAPHAEL: Yet you brought your harp here with you.

Sister Miriam looks at her Superior, surprised.

SISTER MIRIAM: How did you know? I thought I'd hidden it.

MOTHER RAPHAEL: (*laughs*) In the attic? That's the first place we check. You'd be surprised what the postulants smuggle in. Food. Cigarettes. Mascara. Look what I once found up there.

And Mother Raphael removes a cloth to reveal a record player.

MOTHER RAPHAEL: I'd like to hear your voice - before I consign it to the flames.

Sister Miriam looks at it - really quite threatened.

SISTER MIRIAM: As you wish. But may I leave?

And Mother Raphael nods.

MOTHER RAPHAEL: (*trying to remember the quote*) "By the rivers of Babylon we sat and wept when we remembered Zion." Do you remember the rest of that Psalm?

SISTER MIRIAM: (*uneasily*) "There on the willows we hung our harps. For how can we sing God's song while in a foreign land?"

MOTHER RAPHAEL: (*gently*) Even the Jews took their harps down eventually. And sang again.

Sister Miriam looks at Mother Raphael - puzzled.

MOTHER RAPHAEL: Do you think it's just co-incidence that a total stranger gave you this? It might be a sign.

SISTER MIRIAM: Of what? His appalling taste?

MOTHER RAPHAEL: That you're meant to sing once more.

SISTER MIRIAM: (*very threatened*) And pigs, with respect, might start flying backwards. There is nothing left inside me now of - (*points to LP Cover*) - that creature there - or the world that she once lived in.

MOTHER RAPHAEL: Or the man she loved?

SISTER MIRIAM: I do not believe in signs. Everything is gone. And this- (*indicates LP Record*) - is just a piece of plastic. (*with a hint of desperation*) Do I have your permission to destroy it? (*with real urgency*) Please.

And Mother Raphael nods and passes the record to her.

Sister Miriam holds the record up - ready to toss it onto the fire. It is a terrible moment for her. But she hesitates - she cannot bring herself to destroy her own work - or her memories.

Mother Raphael takes the record from her, gently. Mother Raphael walks to the record player, and puts the record on the turntable.

*Soon the sounds of a harp begin, and we hear the voice of Mary O'Hara – on the LP record - singing **Danny Boy**.*

Sister Miriam listens to her voice, as if sitting by the rivers of Babylon, remembering Zion. Perhaps, almost involuntarily, she mouths a few lines from the song she is hearing - a painful echo of a distant, happy time.

59

*One verse of **Danny Boy**, then darkness...*

SCENE TWELVE

Stage left Tyrone is working with a piece of rope, knotting it carefully.

Stage right Sister Miriam is also working with some rope.

As the scene progresses, it becomes clear that Tyrone is making a noose and Sister Miriam is making a halter to put around the (unseen) cow.

Mother Raphael enters with a letter. She looks at the rope, puzzled.

MOTHER RAPHAEL: That looks like fun.

SISTER MIRIAM: A fence came down in the paddock. So I'll have to tie the cow up.

MOTHER RAPHAEL: You've received some mail, Sister Miriam.

SISTER MIRIAM: (*surprised*) But we're not allowed personal letters.

MOTHER RAPHAEL: Perhaps I'd better get the brandy - in case the news is bad.

SISTER MIRIAM: Please Mother - just read it.

MOTHER RAPHAEL: (*opening it, reads*) "Greetings Sister Miriam. This is a note from You Know Who."

SISTER MIRIAM: It's that American - isn't it?

MOTHER RAPHAEL: (*reads*) "Scrape off the chicken shit and brace yourself, Sister" - (*looks up*) Yes - that sounds like him.

MOTHER RAPHAEL: (*continues reading*) "Enclosed please find a medal which I hope you'll wear with pride." (*passing the medal to Miriam*) When did you convert him, Sister Miriam?

SISTER MIRIAM: (*looking at the medal*) Around the time that Joseph Stalin was made into a saint.

Mother Raphael looks at Sister Miriam, puzzled, then continues reading.

MOTHER RAPHAEL: Last night you were awarded the Proletariat Art Medallion. Please accept my congratulations, along with those of Leonard Brezhnev and the Communist Party of South-East Cheam – of which, by the way, you are now a Lifetime Member.

SISTER MIRIAM: (*shocked, mutters*) What?!

MOTHER RAPHAEL: (*looks up, says calmly*) Oh the bishop will be thrilled.

Sister Miriam, meanwhile, is angrily working on the rope, pulling it furiously but having absolutely no success. Tyrone's noose, however, is terrific. Strong, taut, a work of art.

And now we see Tyrone working with his own piece of rope. As he does this, he recites the contents of his letter - although

61

Mother Raphael keeps holding it and mouthing the words
which Tyrone speaks -

TYRONE: PS: My wife made a promise to me once. If *she* died
first, she'd send me a sign that she was in Heaven - and the
sign would be this: for every year that we'd been married,
she would make a rose bloom - in any garden of my
choosing – no matter what season. I gave her my word I'd
test this out. Although it's patently ridiculous - and I'll
always be an atheist - my word is still my word.

TYRONE: So I might as well choose Stanbrook. I'm sure it has
a garden somewhere.

Sister Miriam looks up, alarmed.

TYRONE: On my visit there next week I want four roses in
your garden. Four roses exactly. No more. No less. So this
God of yours better have green thumbs - though judging by
the spuds you grow, I doubt it. Finally – will you make me
a card – a really nice card – with a sycamore leaf on the
front? Inside write the words *Tyrone* and *Jean*. Do a good
job please 'cause I'm going to be buried with it. (*very
firmly but with no self-pity*) I'm sick of people saying what
a great gift Life's supposed to be. (*with great feeling*)
Believe me, lady, it isn't. (*gently, ironically*) Keep away
from those Vikings, OK?

*Then Tyrone pulls hard on the piece of rope and it becomes a
very sinister hangman's noose.*

SISTER MIRIAM: (*to Mother Raphael*) Is there a sender's
name and address?

MOTHER RAPHAEL: (*looking at letter*) Yes. He's Mr Tyrone Kane.

SISTER MIRIAM: Do I have your permission to reply?

MOTHER RAPHAEL: (*sternly*) All right. But no lectures!

Mother Raphael exits. Sister Miriam works away at her knot while she recites her reply.

SISTER MIRIAM: I must warn you - Mr Kane - there will *not* be four roses in the garden at Stanbrook. God is subtle. He does not deliver signs nor respond to threats of suicide. Besides the soil here's *dreadful*. Even the weeds have trouble with it. So prepare yourself for disappointment. I grieve for you and for your wife and for all who die before their time. You were obviously pulling my leg in your letter. Communists indeed!!

Sister Miriam's knot unravels. But Tyrone's knot is tight and ready for when he needs it.

Darkness. On the soundtrack we hear, once again, the **Benedictine Chants***.*

SCENE THIRTEEN

On the screen we see slides of the garden at Stanbrook Abbey. It is bleak and barren and empty - not a rose in sight.

The door to the Visitors' Room opens. Tyrone enters, staggering, not from alcohol but from the weight of a large sack he is carrying across his shoulders. Tyrone deposits the sack near the grille.

Tyrone goes to the rack, pulls out a leaf card and begins to scribble a quick note to Sister Miriam. He reads its contents aloud as he writes.

TYRONE: (*irate*) Sister "M". I've brought you a ten-pound bag of horse shit. Call it a going away present. (*almost casually*) You were right about the roses. There's *nothing* growing out there. (*covering up his disappointment*) Well I wasn't expecting them anyway. To be honest, I'm a bit like you. I don't believe in miracles. So, I guess that's it. Goodbye for good. No prayers for me, OK? I have a right to be forgotten.

Tyrone is about to slide the letter under the grille when there's a noise behind the grille and its little door begins to open.

Tyrone looks up - and is surprised to see Mother Raphael standing in front of him.

MOTHER RAPHAEL: (*surprised to see him*) Our visiting time's over.

TYRONE: Sure. (*indicates Hessian bag*) Just dropping this off.

Then Tyrone notices that Mother Raphael is clutching a single rose.

TYRONE: What's *that*?

MOTHER RAPHAEL: A rose, of course.

TYRONE: Secret admirer, huh?

MOTHER RAPHAEL: Hardly. It's from the garden.

TYRONE: (*threatened*) What garden?

MOTHER RAPHAEL: Our garden.

TYRONE: That's a lie.

MOTHER RAPHAEL: I don't believe we've been introduced.

TYRONE: (*upset*) Listen, Sister, I don't know what you're smoking - but I've seen your garden and it looks like it's been hit by napalm. There's no way *that thing* grew in it!

MOTHER RAPHAEL: Oh it's not from the front garden.

In order to calm Tyrone down, Mother Raphael steers him towards the window and points.

MOTHER RAPHAEL: It came from our compost heap. (*points*) See? We pruned our plants quite hard last year and then tossed the cuttings on it. When I looked this morning, *they* were there.

Tyrone - in amazement and almost terror, stares out the window.

TYRONE: (*softly, in amazement, counts the roses he can see*) Three roses...

MOTHER RAPHAEL: (*happily*) Yes. Plus, this one I just picked of course. That makes -

TYRONE: (*finishes the sentence for her with a shocked whisper*) Four.

Tyrone is so stunned he has to sit down.

MOTHER RAPHAEL: We never get roses at this time of year. Must be all that chicken manure. (*notices the change in Tyrone*) Are you all right?

TYRONE: Sister Miriam - where is she?

MOTHER RAPHAEL: Observing a Silence.

TYRONE: She can look at it some other time. I need her. Now. (*with unexpected desperation*) Please!

MOTHER RAPHAEL: Wait here.

Mother Raphael exits through the grille door - and shuts it behind her.

Tyrone sits, breathing deeply so he won't hyperventilate - then puts his head in his hands and tries to relax. He is struggling to come to terms with the new twist his life is taking.

Then, overwhelmed by agitation, he jumps up and rings the Visitor's Bell loudly.

TYRONE: (*trying to peer through the grille*) Sister Miriam? Sister Miriam?!

SISTER MIRIAM: (*not pleased*) You have no right to interrupt my prayers.

TYRONE: (*almost breathless*) Your garden - four roses.

SISTER MIRIAM: Nonsense.

Tyrone grabs the single rose from the vase and presses it against the grille.

TYRONE: Well get a whiff of this!

SISTER MIRIAM: (*sniffs*) All I can smell is horse business.

So Tyrone moves further along the grille, away from the bag.

Tyrone taps on the grille - to show Sister Miriam where he is.

TYRONE: Up here. Come up here. Now take a snort.

And Sister Miriam presses her face against the grille - to smell the rose that Tyrone is holding.

TYRONE: (*gloating*) It's a rose. And there are three others out there - growing on your compost heap. Go on. Admit it. I actually got a sign!

SISTER MIRIAM: (*defensive*) Oh the heap doesn't count. It's not part of the garden.

TYRONE: (*annoyed*) Of course it counts. Jesus Christ - who's the atheist round here? Four roses bloomed. In the garden. At Stanbrook. Jean's really up there after all. (*stunned*) She's up there watching over me...Oh my God - the things she's seen! Well from now on all that's over. I'm going to straighten out. Buy some clothes - earn some dough. Make me two dozen leaf cards - just to get started.

SISTER MIRIAM: (*not pleased*) And what shall I write on them? Greetings from Moscow?

TYRONE: No. No. Forget the "commies". We have to take this seriously now. We'll put Beatles' lyrics on them and sell them to the swingers. I hope you know the words to "I Want to Hold Your Hand"?

SISTER MIRIAM: (*appalled*) I do not hold hands with strangers, Mr Kane! And I refuse to waste my time making leaf-cards for "swingers". I don't know what "swingers" are exactly - but I don't like the sound of them. You made more sense when you were drunk.

TYRONE: (*trying to make her share his enthusiasm*) OK. No Beatles. You could just write verses - T.S. Eliot and stuff.

SISTER MIRIAM: "Not with a bang but a whimper!" Now isn't that uplifting.

TYRONE: (*hurt*) Why aren't you happy for me? For the first time in years I've got a bit of - hope. To be honest it feels - scary. It's like this rose on the compost heap. It's hard enough for the thing to grow without you trampling all over it.

Sister Miriam knows that he is right.

SISTER MIRIAM: (*gently but realistically*) Prophets get signs and saints get signs. Not people like you and me. I have to go. I'm late.

TYRONE: (*desperately*) Wait! Please! There are lots of other poems. I saw one in this book last night. I even wrote some of it down. (*takes paper out of his pocket, tries to read but cannot decipher his own writing*) Oh, Christ! I must have been drunker than I thought.

SISTER MIRIAM: (*heading off-stage*) Please close the door properly when you -

TYRONE: (*reading aloud from the sheet of paper*) "Redemption, like our janitor, comes when we go home -"

Sister Miriam stops dead in her tracks - shocked - literally - as if struck by lightning. Did she really hear that?

Tyrone cannot see Sister Miriam of course. So he has no idea of the devastating effect this quote has just had on her.

TYRONE: (*continues to read*) "- a stooped man turning out the lights." (*looking up from the paper*) I kind of understand it, too. (*pauses*) Sister Miriam? Are you there?

No reply. Tyrone thinks she has gone. So he takes the rose from the vase, then turns and heads for the door.

As he is going - from behind the grille -

SISTER MIRIAM: (*struggling to stay calm*) Where did you happen to read that?

TYRONE: If you don't like it I'm sure there are -

SISTER MIRIAM: Where?

TYRONE: (*confessing awkwardly*) Eileen keeps this book beside her bed - Popular Poets of the Twentieth Century.

SISTER MIRIAM: (*desperate to know*) And that was in the book?

TYRONE: (*embarrassed as he confesses*) Yeah. We didn't do it - if it's any consolation. I was too sloshed and she's a bit - hey - why am I telling a nun about my sex life?

SISTER MIRIAM: (*trying desperately to sound calm*) Do you remember the poet's name?

TYRONE: Nah. They had a photo of him though. Dark looking. Handsome. Dead, of course.

SISTER MIRIAM: (*gently*) Yes. Of course.

Tyrone suspects that Sister Miriam is interested - but he hasn't got a clue why. Meanwhile, on the soundtrack we begin to hear the hauntingly beautiful chorus from "Song for Athene" by John Tavener. It gradually grows louder as the scene progresses.

TYRONE: "Redemption - like our janitor -" You could fit that on a leaf-card. You like it, don't you? Sister Miriam?

Sister Miriam stands facing the grille. Her voice remains calm but she is now wiping her eyes quickly with the backs of her hands - as she says -

SISTER MIRIAM: (*as if not too impressed any more*) It's all right I suppose. But wouldn't Redemption turn on the lights?

And a bell starts ringing in the distance.

TYRONE: I think that means you have to go.

SISTER MIRIAM: It's only evening prayers. I'll tell them I was busy.

Tyrone cannot see this but as he talks, Sister Miriam crouches on the floor, buries her face in her hands and sobs desperately, but as quietly as possible. The chorus, by now, is quite audible and increasing in volume.

TYRONE: (*eagerly, happily*) Great! Now here's the deal. We've got to start early - so we'll make the Christmas rush. On every card you write a verse - Silent Night for the Mums and Dads - and bits of Das Kapital for the Commies. Or maybe you could draw them a hammer and sickle - with a Santa's hat on it.

TYRONE: (*a bit worried when she doesn't bite his head off for this suggestion*) Are you listening to me Sister Miriam? (*tapping on grille*) Hello in there? We need to have some forward planning. I can't do everything on my own. Sister Miriam? Sister Miriam?

But Sister Miriam does not reply. Instead she sobs as quietly as she can, covering her mouth with her veil, completely undone by this unexpected "sign" she has just received.

Tyrone keeps calling her name. But the chorus is so loud is almost drowns out his voice.

And soon this singing has overwhelmed Tyrone's cries and Sister Miriam's weeping - as if reminding us all of the power of Destiny and the helplessness of unsuspecting mortals.

Gradual darkness.

INTERVAL

71

SCENE FOURTEEN

*On the soundtrack we hear the joyful voice of the Mary O'Hara singing a verse or two from **The Frog's Wedding**.*

A nervous Tyrone stands in a spotlight. He looks at the audience - like he is struggling to remember his lines. Then he clears his throat and says -

TYRONE: An Irishman enters a pub, orders 3 glasses of Guinness, then lines them up on the bar - and takes a sip out of each until all 3 glasses are empty. The barman sees this and says to the Irishman - "Why don't you just order 1 glass at a time?"

As Tyrone speaks, it becomes clear that, in spite of his nerves, he looks better dressed; he's had a shave and his clothes are neat and tidy.

TYRONE: And the Irishman replies - "Well - you see - I have 2 brothers. One's in America and one's in Australia and I'm drinking like this so that I can remember the nights when we all drank together." Next day the Irishman returns to the pub - but this time he only orders 2 glasses of beer. The barman notices and says - "Please accept my sympathies for your tragic loss. Which one of your brothers has died?" And the Irishman replies - "Oh no, nobody's dead. I decided to quit drinking."

Then Tyrone looks at the audience and says - very awkwardly -

TYRONE: My name is Tyrone. (*with great effort*) And I'm an alcoholic. I've been sober now almost 30 days.

And on the soundtrack we hear -

AA VOICES: (Voices only) Hi Tyrone!!

Darkness...

SCENE FIFTEEN

On screen the words "New York, 1957."

Richard Selig is standing in a doorway. He looks very pale and ill.

Mary enters and looks at him with concern.

RICHARD: (*leaning against the door, exhausted*) I don't know why they call it a "heat-wave". A wave means movement and there's not a breeze outside.

YOUNG MARY: Where have you been?

RICHARD: Downstairs. To get the mail.

YOUNG MARY: You've been gone for three hours.

RICHARD: I came back through Manhattan. (*proudly*) On the subway. And I didn't faint once.

YOUNG MARY: You're supposed to rest after radiation treatments. The doctor was quite specific.

Meanwhile Mary removes Richard's shirt, sponges him down, then replaces the shirt with a pyjama top - like an experienced nurse.

RICHARD: There was a letter for me. From Viking Books. They don't think "Redemption" could ever be a janitor.

YOUNG MARY: (*hurt for him but hiding it*) What do publishers know? Send it somewhere else.

RICHARD: There are no others left in the phone book - apart from Zebra Press - and they only do comics. So now we are officially starving.

YOUNG MARY: Then I'll get a job.

RICHARD: (*hopefully*) Singing?

YOUNG MARY: Remember what my agent said? There are millions of singers in America already. So I might be a waitress. (*trying to sound pleased about it*) It'll make a nice change.

RICHARD: (*as Mary undresses him*) Do you love me?

YOUNG MARY: Of course.

RICHARD: I don't know why. I've ruined your career. If you'd stayed on in London you'd still be successful. But now you don't even have a harp.

YOUNG MARY: (*lying*) And I don't mind a bit. Twenty-nine guineas to ship it here from England! The cheek of P&O. I'm glad I sold it. Besides, if a man is feeling poorly he belongs in his own country. And I love New York. I'll not hear a word against it.

RICHARD: (*eagerly*) Mary - I've just done something wicked - something that will anger you very much.

And Richard starts to cough. Mary wipes his face and tries to make him a bit more comfortable.

YOUNG MARY: Did you tell off the landlord?

RICHARD: (*with his head down the toilet*) Worse.

YOUNG MARY: You didn't have alcohol?

RICHARD: Much worse.

Mary, meanwhile, helps him on with his pyjama pants. Richard is too weak now to do it himself. Then Mary helps Richard to his feet.

RICHARD: Your Dad sent us one hundred dollars.

YOUNG MARY: (*astonished, relieved*) Oh - God love him. We can pay our rent.

RICHARD: I spent it. Every cent. That's my sin. (*proudly*) It's a beauty, isn't it?

YOUNG MARY: (*reminding herself he's ill & keeping her temper in check*) Not at all. Whatever you bought, I'll take it straight back.

RICHARD: Aren't you even curious?

YOUNG MARY: (*lying*) Not a bit.

RICHARD: I took your Dad's money and went to Manhattan. To all the musical instrument shops. I showed them your photo.

YOUNG MARY: (*worried*) Whatever for?

RICHARD: So they could tell me if they'd seen you. They remembered you clearly on West 54th Street. "A regular," the lady says. "She comes in here twice a week - and looks - but never ever buys." So I asked to see just what you'd been looking at - (*almost accusingly*) - the double-action Erard Concert harp with plectrum.

Mary looks at Richard, stunned. He has just exposed a deep and buried desire.

RICHARD: It's downstairs - in the lobby. I dragged it here myself.

YOUNG MARY: (*struggling to hide her feelings*) Spending our last cent on a silly concert harp. I've never heard the like. I hope you kept the docket. I'm returning it right now. Why did you do it?

RICHARD: (*calmly*) Because I wanted to leave you something, Mary - something you liked - so you'd always remember me.

YOUNG MARY: Gosh you make me angry sometimes. You aren't going to die. It will not happen.

She is just about to start weeping when -

RICHARD: Come on. Don't start. Here - blow your nose.

And Richard thrusts a piece of paper at her.

And Mary looks at the piece of paper - astonished.

YOUNG MARY: Richard - this is a telegram.

RICHARD: (*casually*) Oh yes. It was in with the letters. That lazy delivery boy won't climb the stairs. (*as if it's of no consequence*) It's from a Mr Ed Sullivan. He wants you to go on some television show. (*calmly*) But I'll ring him and tell him that you'd rather be a waitress.

And Mary looks at Richard in astonishment.

Darkness. Then from the darkness the Voice of Ed Sullivan can be heard saying -

ED SULLIVAN: (Voice Only) My next guest has already won thousands of admirers in England and Ireland. And tonight, ladies and gentlemen, she's going to sing for us a number from the smash-hit Broadway show - The Fantasticks. Right here on our stage, ladies and gentlemen, is the lovely Miss Mary O'Hara.

Applause. Then Mary steps into the spotlight and sings the achingly beautiful **Try to Remember***.*

SCENE SIXTEEN

Sister Miriam is standing on one side of the grille, lost in memories of her life in New York with Richard.

Tyrone stands on the other side of the grille, clean-shaven, neatly dressed, a little strung out from the pressures of sobriety, yet also pleased with his progress.

TYRONE: Hello in there! A customer's waiting!

SISTER MIRIAM: (*shaken out of her memories*) Mr Kane? Are you all right? You sound a little bit - sober.

TYRONE: (*bashfully*) Yeah. I am.

SISTER MIRIAM: Congratulations. Now isn't that something! You must be feeling wonderful.

TYRONE: I feel like I've swallowed barbed wire.

SISTER MIRIAM: (*encouraging*) Your wife would have been extremely proud.

TYRONE: (*gently*) Don't say that. Please. (*with real regret*) She'd be so ashamed if she could see me now.

SISTER MIRIAM: Maybe she'd feel honoured.

TYRONE: Honoured? That her husband turned into a drunk?

SISTER MIRIAM: That you loved her so much you had no life without her.

Tyrone looks at the grille - surprised by this insight.

TYRONE: You always cheer me up, you know. And I've had a real stinker of a week. I'm up to Step 9 on the AA Programme.

SISTER MIRIAM: I'm not sure what that means exactly. Not many of the Sisters here are recovering alcoholics.

TYRONE: Step 9's when you apologise for all the wrongs you've done to others. Last night I addressed a hall full of Communists. I confessed that the money they'd been spending on leaf-cards had actually gone to a convent of nuns who prayed each night for the conversion of Russia!...You run much faster when you're sober.

SISTER MIRIAM: And is that why you've come here today? To apologise to me?

TYRONE: Hell, no! You're the only person in my life I've never really hurt. (*eagerly*) I'm here because I showed your cards to one of the guys at AA. He owns a gallery in Knightsbridge. Called "Adrian's". Even you must have heard of it. It's always in the papers.

SISTER MIRIAM: Not in The Catholic Weekly.

TYRONE: (*proudly*) Well he thinks - Sister Miriam - that you're seriously talented.

SISTER MIRIAM: (*laughs*) Is that what people call Art these days - dead leaves glued on to bits of paper?

TYRONE: (*almost rebuking her*) Your cards have been adored - so far - by derelicts, drunks and Communists. Why that's practically the whole of British society. No wonder Adrian's desperate to meet you.

SISTER MIRIAM: Well it's out of the question.

TYRONE: Why? (*sensing her reluctance*) Would it be so bad if he purchased a few - whacked them in frames - then held an exhibition? You'll probably end up famous!

SISTER MIRIAM: (*very threatened*) I don't want to be famous.

TYRONE: (*hurt*) Most artists would kill for a chance like this.

SISTER MIRIAM: I am not an artist.

TYRONE: Well Adrian disagrees. He assures me you have a - a genius for texture. (*trying to reason with her*) And I hate to see that talent of yours just - buried - in this Abbey. Why do you want to hide here anyway?

It's a question too close to the bone.

SISTER MIRIAM: (*stung*) We get so sick of hearing that - that we've come to this convent to hide. What have we got to hide behind? We don't have liquor - drugs - or sex - no radio - television - music or make-up. There is nothing to distract us here. Just silence. And you cannot hide from silence. Ask any prisoner in any jail what it's like to be left with yourself.

TYRONE: All right. I apologise. But let me bring Adrian here - to meet you. It's no big deal - people do it all the time - introduce their friends to one another.

SISTER MIRIAM: (*almost begging him*) Please. Don't.

TYRONE: (*getting worried about her*) What's wrong with you today, Sister Miriam? You sound like your normal abrasive self - but - but something else is going on. (*with concern*) Now tell me what it is.

SISTER MIRIAM: I'm not permitted to discuss it.

TYRONE: Says who? Isn't that what friends are for - to talk your problems over with?

No reply.

TYRONE: We are friends aren't we, Sister Miriam?

SISTER MIRIAM: (*gently, not angrily*) We aren't allowed to have friends in here. Friends are like mirrors. They reflect ourselves. I'm sorry - but I have to go... Goodbye.

TYRONE: (*worried about her*) Sister Miriam - please - come back! Remember what your leaflet said - you should never end a visit in an upset state of mind! (*calls*) Sister Miriam! (*exasperated, yells*) Women!

Darkness...

SCENE SEVENTEEN

On screen the words "Fire Island, New York, 1957".

On the soundtrack we hear the "Maria" chorus from "A Song for Athene".

Mary and Richard have been on a camping trip. Now they are packing up to go home. Richard is very weak so Mary does most of the work.

A storm is approaching in the distance.

Richard holds up a jar filled with muddy water.

YOUNG MARY: What's in there?

RICHARD: Just some tadpoles. I caught them while you were swimming.

YOUNG MARY: You can't take tadpoles on a plane.

81

RICHARD: Why not? I'll ask the stewardess to mind them.

YOUNG MARY: They give out tea and coffee. They do not mind pets - especially slimy ones.

RICHARD: (*wistfully*) When I was a boy I thought it amazing that these little things could turn into frogs. For a while I believed that all of us could grow more legs - or a few extra heads - and become something different.

YOUNG MARY: (*playfully*) Really? And what would I turn into?

RICHARD: You?

YOUNG MARY: Yes.

RICHARD: Well - let's see - (*quite seriously*) - you're not very bright - and there are other girls more beautiful - but when I watch you walk along the sand - your hair all blown - and your feet so light they hardly leave prints - you remind me of a maiden in an old Irish ballad.
(*smiles wistfully*) Remember on our honeymoon - on that beach at Arran Island - you started singing to the waves - and all those heads popped up from the sea - fifteen of them rolled ashore and settled at your feet.

YOUNG MARY: (*sitting beside him*) They were only seals. Seals love high notes.

RICHARD: They were Selkies - from the depths. And as they gathered round you, I thought to myself "Dear God in Heaven, who have I married? Is this woman mortal?" (*quite seriously*) You'll turn into something wonderful, Mary - when the time comes.

YOUNG MARY: (*resolutely*) I am Mrs Richard Selig and I'll not be changing any more. The life I have is enchanted enough.

RICHARD: I'm sure the tadpole thinks so too. But four legs still appear.

YOUNG MARY: (*has just finished packing*) That's it. Let's go. If we hurry we might beat the storm.

But Richard does not move.

YOUNG MARY: But you'll have to carry the tadpoles. To be perfectly honest those poor little creatures will not be happy in New York. (*stops, looks at him, realises that something is wrong*) Richard?

RICHARD: (*almost casually*) Mary - love - just at this moment I'd rather stay here.

Mary touches Richard's forehead. He's burning up. He tries to stand but cannot.

YOUNG MARY: Yes - yes. Of course. You lie there now and take your time.

RICHARD: I'll be all right if I can just close my eyes.

Suddenly a loud thunderclap rocks the stage.

YOUNG MARY: (*hugging him tightly*) Richard? Richard? (*gently but desperately*) Don't leave me.

RICHARD: I'll have to go eventually. Remember what the doctor said. We have to prepare ourselves.

YOUNG MARY: (*lying*) And I'm trying. I am. (*desperately*) But not now. Please.

RICHARD: Don't forget what I taught you - about paying the bills. When you write a cheque, sign it "Mrs Richard Selig" - but if I'm dead you're to put the words "Mrs Mary Selig."

YOUNG MARY: I'll always be Mrs Richard Selig. Always.

RICHARD: (*touching her face proudly*) There's not much point if I'm not here.

YOUNG MARY: Then I won't let you go. (*fiercely*) I'll hold you to this earth and to this life. I can do it!!

RICHARD: I'll bet you can...

Richard struggles, unsuccessfully, to stand up.

YOUNG MARY: You musn't move.

RICHARD: But we'll miss our flight.

YOUNG MARY: (*trying to be brave*) So what. It's only a plane. We can always get the Greyhound.

RICHARD: It's Sunday night. The buses are packed. I've ruined our trip. I'm sorry.

YOUNG MARY: I've never heard such nonsense. There'll be seats down the back of the bus. The nuns at school always used to say that the back of the bus was reserved for the wicked.

RICHARD: Why?

YOUNG MARY: There are more vibrations near the wheels. And if a girl isn't careful she might just get a thrill. So missing a plane has a few advantages.

RICHARD: (*tenderly*) You always make me laugh.

Very loud thunder. They both jump in fright.

YOUNG MARY: (*gently covering him and rocking him*) I'm here, my darling. Nothing can harm you. Nothing...Nothing...

Mary does her best to hide her terror - because they are totally exposed in the storm.

Richard looks up at her, weak and sick.

RICHARD: Will you sing that song - the one I taught you?

YOUNG MARY: Don't be silly. There's a storm on.

A sudden and terrifying flash of lightning.

YOUNG MARY: (*protecting Richard but trying to sound casual*) That was a bright one, wasn't it?

RICHARD: What was, Mary?... Oh God - I can't see!

For the first time in his life, Richard panics.

RICHARD: (*frantically*) Mary - are you there?

And Mary looks at Richard. His eyes are open wide. She runs her hand across his eyes. But Richard doesn't even blink. And she realises that he is now blind.

YOUNG MARY: (*hiding her terror*) It's all right now. The worst is over. Ssshh...Ssshh.

And Mary begins to sing very gently as she cradles Richard -

YOUNG MARY: (*sings*) "I gave my love a cherry, without a stone..."

And Mary sings the song for Richard - and does her best to shelter her husband from the huge storm raging over them.

On the screen we see the following newspaper headline - Plane Crashes in Storm. 200 Die. Irish Singer & Husband Miss Flight.

(This really did happen.)

SCENE EIGHTEEN

Tyrone stands over his telephone. He hesitates, then picks it up and dials a number.

TYRONE: (*into phone*) Eileen? You'll never guess who this is. (*beat*) (*with urgency*) Wait - please! Before you hang up - (*awkwardly*) I just rang to tell you that I've joined this club - very exclusive - kind of like the Masons - only harder to get into. You only qualify for membership if you've ruined your life and lost all your friends. No, Eileen, it's not Scientology.

(*with effort*) I'm in A.A. (*pause, then -*) Not Amway. A.A.
And I didn't phone to sell you something! As part of my
rehab I have to ring up anyone I've ever vomited on, lied to
or been impotent with. So, how are you?

As Eileen talks, Tyrone's expression reveals shame and
embarrassment.

TYRONE: Yeah...Yeah...You're absolutely right. And you
know what the worst of it is, Eileen? I was too damn drunk
to appreciate you.
(*pause*) No. It's true. You saw me at my lowest - at the
bottom of my life - and you never turned away. You never
once gave up on me. There's no way I can thank you for
that. (*sincerely*) You're a credit to Stalin, Eileen. (*tenderly*)
Goodbye.

Tyrone hangs up. It's all too hard. He reaches down and pulls a
bottle of whiskey from under his bed. Tyrone is just about
to open it when his phone rings.

TYRONE: (*answering phone*) Hello? (*pause*) Bolshoi Ballet?
Sure, I'd love to! I'll see you in half an hour. Oh, Eileen -
do you know anyone who wants a bottle of Johnny
Walker?

Darkness. On the soundtrack we hear "The Beast in Me" by
Nick Lowe.

SCENE NINETEEN

On screen the words October 14th, 1957.

Richard is lying in his hospital bed. He has just woken up from a fitful doze.

Young Mary is sitting close by him.

As the scene progresses, we also become aware of Sister Miriam kneeling in prayer, remembering this night.

RICHARD: Mary?

YOUNG MARY: (*very gently*) Yes?

RICHARD: What time is it?

YOUNG MARY: Ten past two. In the morning.

RICHARD: You should go home.

YOUNG MARY: The hospital said I could sleep here tonight. Wasn't that nice of them?

Mary picks up Richard's hand - and presses it against her cheek.

RICHARD: You're frowning, aren't you? What are you thinking?

YOUNG MARY: Nothing.

RICHARD: We've never had secrets. Don't start now.

YOUNG MARY: I was wishing we'd caught that plane that crashed. I was wishing we'd died together.

RICHARD: And not have that wonderful bus trip?! I never thought the nuns could tell me how to improve my sex life.

(*senses Mary's wretchedness, reassuringly*) Mary - listen - I'm glad we missed that flight. Because I want you to keep on living.

YOUNG MARY: I don't think I'll be strong enough.

RICHARD: (*almost happily*) What you and I have created together won't end in death. The worst that's going to happen is we might be parted for a few dozen years. So what? In the scheme of things that's the blink of an eye. Why it isn't as long as a trip to Manhattan - and you can go to Manhattan without getting weepy.
(*holding her hand*) The one great enterprise in this world is to learn how to love and keep loving. And we will. Forever and ever. (*calmly, almost bossy*) Now I'd like you to sing me to sleep. But first of all tell me what you did tonight? And you're not allowed to use the words doctor, hospital or enema.

YOUNG MARY: Well - let's see. I went to Mass while you were resting.

RICHARD: Did you go to the park?

YOUNG MARY: (*eager to take his mind off his suffering*) Oh, yes. Richard it has the cheekiest squirrels - typical New Yorkers - they come right to your feet and demand their chestnuts. One of them had the meanest black eyes - I thought he was going to mug me.

RICHARD: (*too weak to shout but shocked by the intensity of a sudden, sharp pain*) Oh God - God help me!

YOUNG MARY: (*rising*) I'll get the doctor.

But Richard raises his hand to stop her.

RICHARD: (*sensing his death his imminent*) No...You're not allowed to say the word doctor. You promised.

YOUNG MARY: Please -

RICHARD: Sit down, Mary. Just us...Just us...Where's your hand. I need your hand. (*trying to conquer his pain, and with real urgency*) I want to hear about the park.

So Mary respects her husband's wishes. She sits on the bed, clutching Richard's hand, and nursing his head and chest in her arms.

Richard looks up at her as she talks. His eyes remain wide open the whole time.

YOUNG MARY: (*calmly continues*) They've strung these lights - these coloured lights - in all the trees and bushes. And when the sun went down the strangest thing happened. The lights came on - and a bird went wild - whooshing its wings and crying out and fleeing the tree in panic. And I thought of you - and what a poem it would make - and how cleverly you'd write it -

Young Mary begins to suspect that , even though Richard is still looking at her, he has actually died. But she continues talking without changing the tone of her voice so she won't disturb his soul as it slips away.

YOUNG MARY: - describing that bird - how it flew away - leaving nothing behind but its shadow on the grass.

And she continues to talk - calmly, tenderly -

YOUNG MARY: "Peter has come and Paul has come. James has come and John has come. Martha and Mary Virgin have come. And Jesus Christ the Mild has come. To bestow on thee their affection and love. To bestow on thee their affection and love."

Then Young Mary closes Richard's eyes slowly with her fingers. And as she holds him, Young Mary tries to sing for him as she promised -

YOUNG MARY: (*sings falteringly*)
My young love said to me -
My mother won't mind
And my father won't slight you
For your lack of kind.
And he stepped away from me
and this he did say-
"It will not be long love,
till our wedding day."

Young Mary cannot finish the song. The enormity of her loss completely overwhelms her. And she rocks Richard's body and sobs and sobs.

But Sister Miriam, who is watching, and remembering, continues it - and manages to finish the song she started seventeen years earlier.

SISTER MIRIAM: (*sings*)
He stepped away from me
and he moved through the fair
And fondly I watched him
move here and move there
and then he went onward
with one star awake

as the swan in the evening
moved over the lake.

*As Sister Miriam sings, Young Mary removes her coat to reveal a
black dress underneath. She places the coat over Richard's
face and body, picks up a rose and walks to the centre of
the stage where an oblong light reveals his grave. Young
Mary places the rose on the grave, then drops to the
ground, sobbing helplessly...*

SISTER MIRIAM:
Last night he came to me
my dead love came in
so softly he came that
his feet made no din
and he lay in and on me
and this he did say -
"It will not be long love
till our wedding day."

Darkness...

SCENE TWENTY

*Tyrone is shaving. He is also wearing a towel with a large, red
hammer and sickle on it.*

*A Woman's Voice calls out at Tyrone's front door. It belongs to
Eileen, Tyrone's lady-friend. Eileen is very English and
very well-spoken - but we never, of course, see her.*

EILEEN: (Voice Only) (*brightly*) Hellyo! (*Hello*) Anyone
home? Hellyo!

TYRONE; Who's there?

EILEEN: It's I. Eileen.

TYRONE: Oh - hang on.

Tyrone tries to open the door, but it is locked from the inside. He fumbles in his pocket for the key.

TYRONE: (*mutters*) Can't find my key. (*mutters*) I never locked it when I drank.

So Eileen has to talk on the other side of the door as Tyrone crawls around looking for the key.

EILEEN: (Voice Only) Musn't worry.

TYRONE: It's round here somewhere.

EILEEN: (Voice Only) Had a smashing time last night. Isn't it marvellous to wake up sober!

TYRONE: Yeah. Marvellous.

EILEEN: (Voice Only) You know what I was thinking Tyrone? Why should the Bolshoi have all the fun? Perhaps - next time - you and I could do the dancing.

TYRONE: (*looks up in horror*) Dancing?! (*and bangs his head again, then rolls around the floor muttering - so Eileen won't hear*) Shit-shit-shit-shit-shit.

EILEEN: (Voice Only) (*brightly*) Yes. The Workers' Club has a super band. And modern dancing isn't hard. One shuts one's eyes and just pretends one's having an epileptic fit.

93

TYRONE: (*wiping foam from his mouth*) I'd rather have a fit than dance.

EILEEN: (Voice Only) Wonderful. I'll pick you up at 8 then. (*as she departs*) Too-ra, Tyrone! Too-ra!

Tyrone, meanwhile, has been wiping his foamy hands on the cushion of a chair - or whatever - and has discovered the door key underneath.

Tyrone races to the door - and calls out -

TYRONE: Eileen! Wait! Eileen? (*mutters with grim determination*) No way. No way. The dame doesn't exist who can make me dance.

*And Tyrone walks back to resume his shaving. He flicks on the radio - for a bit of music. Soon Gary Glitter can be heard singing - **I Love You, You Love Me**.*

As Tyrone shaves, he begins to tap a foot or move - swaying perhaps - just a little. Then he wriggles his bottom - then his torso - and - well in no time at all - without even trying - he has begun to dance pretty wildly but extremely well. And soon this turns into an impromptu almost-Full Monty as Tyrone gyrates, wiggles his bum once or twice in time to the music, then rips off the towel to reveal - a pair of boxer shorts underneath.

Then a Male Voice - very deep and tough - calls out -

MALE VOICE: Hey - you down there - the piss-pot - turn that bubble-gum garbage off!

Tyrone walks to the window and calls out -

TYRONE: (*angrily*) Hey you! Yes you - the transvestite - screw you!!

MALE VOICE: (*angrily*) Come up here and say that!

TYRONE: (*challenging*) You come down here - or can't you do stairs in stilettos?

We hear sounds of very angry, very heavy feet - clearly not in stilettos, more like army boots - and a door slamming.

Tyrone looks just a little bit worried.

Darkness...

SCENE TWENTY-ONE

Sister Miriam is painting a wall of the attic at Stanbrook Abbey.

Mother Raphael enters. She has a brandy bottle concealed beneath her habit.

Sister Miriam is about to stop painting - out of respect for her Superior - but Mother Raphael motions to her to continue.

MOTHER RAPHAEL: The Stanbrook attic was painted last by Sister Anselma in 1946. She urges you to move the brush- (*indicates by gesture*) - up and down - not side to side.

SISTER MIRIAM: (*quietly amused*) Please thank her for her advice.

MOTHER RAPHAEL: You can thank her yourself. She's coming up later to inspect your work.

95

SISTER MIRIAM: (*puzzled*) Mother she's - (*hesitates*)

MOTHER RAPHAEL: Blind? Yes. So don't be surprised if she puts finger marks everywhere.

Sister Miriam glances up from the painting - and notices the bottle.

SISTER MIRIAM: (*nervously*) Is that brandy?

And Mother Raphael nods.

SISTER MIRIAM: (*worried*) But you only bring the bottle out when a Sister gets - overwhelming news.

MOTHER RAPHAEL: (*gestures at her to continue her painting*) Don't stop - or the undercoat will dry.

So Sister Miriam paints obediently - and tries to remain calm. But after a few seconds, the tension is too much.

SISTER MIRIAM: Has my Father died? Please tell me.

MOTHER RAPHAEL: No one has died - or been hurt or is ill. The world still spins in its God-given orbit with all of us on board.

SISTER MIRIAM: (*looking at brandy*) Then why have you brought the brandy?

But Mother Raphael gestures to Sister Miriam to keep painting.

MOTHER RAPHAEL: How much sleep do you have at night, Sister Miriam? One hour? Two? You live without joy. You have Death in your eyes. When one of my Sisters despairs of Life, it means I've failed her.

SISTER MIRIAM: But -

MOTHER RAPHAEL: (*puts her hand up - no interruptions*) - and steps must be taken. If your memories are killing you, it's best for you to face them - to look them in the eye. Your father has written to say that Decca is trying to find you.

SISTER MIRIAM: (*astonished and relieved*) Decca? The record company?

MOTHER RAPHAEL: (*nods*) They've been hounding him day and night. They want to find out what's become of you. Your LPs are selling so well, they want you to sing again. (*offering the brandy*) I hope this hasn't upset you.

SISTER MIRIAM: (*relieved*) For a moment I thought it might have been important.

Sister Miriam resumes her painting. Mother Raphael looks at the tumbler of brandy, shrugs - then downs it quickly while Sister Miriam's back is turned.

MOTHER RAPHAEL: (*almost annoyed*) Aren't you even a tiny bit flattered? Have you no ego left at all?

SISTER MIRIAM: I'm not Mary O'Hara now, Mother. I don't sing anymore.

MOTHER RAPHAEL: But if you could?

SISTER MIRIAM: It's out of the question. Decca's in London. And no nun has left Stanbrook in 400 years.

MOTHER RAPHAEL: (*more firmly*) But if you could?

No reply.

MOTHER RAPHAEL: A Sister may leave Stanbrook for any procedure that's necessary in order to save her life - such as hospital or dentists or -

SISTER MIRIAM: It would only make things - worse.

MOTHER RAPHAEL: Since everything else appears to have failed, I think it's time we tried desperate measures.

SISTER MIRIAM: I couldn't play. I haven't practised for years.

MOTHER RAPHAEL: Then you must start. And right away. It's time to redeem your harp, Sister Miriam. Go over there now and look at it. And after you've looked at it, play it.

SISTER MIRIAM: But the painting?

MOTHER RAPHAEL: Sister Anselma can finish that.

SISTER MIRIAM: She's blind.

MOTHER RAPHAEL: So? Beethoven was deaf - and that didn't stop him. Just keep her away from the window panes. *(firmly)* You must work on your harp each day for an hour.

SISTER MIRIAM: But -

MOTHER RAPHAEL: (*starting to feel the alcohol*) We are going to heal these wounds of yours - even if it kills you and turns me into a drunk. (*indicating harp*) Come along and help me move it. (*as they shift the harp together*) I'll never understand why God created Love. It's probably ruined more lives than war. If you want me, I'll be in the courtyard - walking off the brandy. (*sternly*) I expect to hear music.

Mother Raphael knows that this will be a very painful and private moment for Sister Miriam. So Mother Raphael exits - but remains within ear-shot.

Sister Miriam looks at the harp covered by the tarpaulin. She begins to remove the tarpaulin very slowly, nervously. She touches it gently and sadly.

*Sister Miriam plucks a string, plucks another, and begins to do some singing scales. And now Sister Miriam's scales gradually become a song - a foot-tapping Gaelic song - joyous and very entertaining - called **Haigh Didil Dum**.*

Sister Miriam is soon carried away by the joy of the song and the sound of her long-dormant voice. She stands up and walks down the stairs, singing joyfully.

We now see Mother Raphael listening. Mother Raphael is so pleased and relieved by what she hears that she is hardly aware of pouring - and drinking - yet another brandy. Mother Raphael then exits happily.

On the screen above, we see the words: Feast of Saint Walburga of Buckfast, Virgin & Martyr.

At the same time, Tyrone enters. His nose is covered by a large, white bandage.

Sister Miriam continues singing as she passes the Visitors' Grille. But she stops when Tyrone says -

TYRONE: (*almost accusingly*) Someone sounds happy.

Tyrone is standing in the Visiting Room with a white bandage over his nose.

SISTER MIRIAM: (*caught off-guard*) Oh - Mr Kane. (*suddenly self-conscious*) Yes I - I suppose I am a little - elated. But it's a very big Feast Day. Saint Walburga of Buckfast. I think we discussed her once.

TYRONE: (*dryly*) The name rings a bell.

SISTER MIRIAM: (*sniffs and is impressed by what she smells*) You smell different.

TYRONE: Oh - that's Brut. (*tries to sniff himself*) Comrade Eileen gave it to me. She says after- shaves are a bourgeois decadence - but I sweat a bit when we dance.

SISTER MIRIAM: (*surprised*) Dance? You??

TYRONE: Why not? (*puts up his arms and pretends to be dancing*) You can do lots of things when your liver grows back.

TYRONE: (*proudly*) We went to this club - and guess what?

SISTER MIRIAM: You got drunk again?

TYRONE: No. No. Something much more frightening. I actually enjoyed myself.

SISTER MIRIAM: Mr Kane, that's wonderful.

TYRONE: Of course it won't last.

SISTER MIRIAM: Why not? Stranger things have happened.

TYRONE: Name one. (*challenging*) Go on. I bet you can't.

SISTER MIRIAM: Um - (*hesitates, then takes the bait*) I'm going to London. (*smugly*) There!

TYRONE: (*astonished*) You?

SISTER MIRIAM: Yes.

TYRONE: But you're in for Life - without parole. And you're not allowed out - unless you're ill. (*with genuine concern*) You're not sick, are you? Sister Miriam?

SISTER MIRIAM: (*calmly*) Goodness no. Decca Records want me to make an LP. They have a studio in London.

A pause. And then Tyrone starts laughing -

TYRONE: (*very amused*) You're a damn fine liar. I almost believed that.

SISTER MIRIAM: I am good, aren't I? I shouldn't make jokes. But I'm a little light headed. It's Lent. And I'm fasting.

TYRONE: Here - have one of these.

And Tyrone drops something into the grille's Visitors' drawer.

And Sister Miriam picks it up.

SISTER MIRIAM: (*shocked*) Mr Kane! This looks like a - a chocolate.

TYRONE: It's a hazelnut whirl. I eat them all day since I've given up smoking. (*tempting her*) Go on. Be wicked. Have one for St. Walburga.

SISTER MIRIAM: (*looking at the chocolate, greatly tempted*) You are the Devil. You're the Devil himself.

TYRONE: (*eating his chocolate loudly, with relish, on the other side of the grille, just centimetres from her*) Mmm...yum...

And it is all too much for Sister Miriam.

SISTER MIRIAM: (*her will-power crumbling*) You're as bad as those Vikings.

She takes a bite.

So does Tyrone.

And they both eat their chocolates - and talk. Relaxed - yet intimate - because they cannot see each other.

TYRONE: (*casually*) Do you ever regret not having children?

SISTER MIRIAM: Sometimes. The Sisters call it "pram ache". Can I have another chocolate?

TYRONE: (*reproachfully*) I thought it was Lent.

SISTER MIRIAM: Yes. But now I've sinned, I can go the whole hog. All I confess to is "eating chocolates". No one ever asks how many.

So Tyrone drops something into the drawer.

And Sister Miriam retrieves it.

SISTER MIRIAM: (*softly but surprised*) This isn't a hazelnut whirl, Mr Kane.

TYRONE: Do you like it?

SISTER MIRIAM: It's beautiful - but -

TYRONE: It was my grandmother's.

SISTER MIRIAM: It looks like...an engagement ring.

TYRONE: Yeah. (*nervously, bashfully*) I've got "pram ache", Sister Miriam. I want to have children. I want to re-marry. So I've decided to ask the only woman in the world who'll put up with me.

A pause - then -

SISTER MIRIAM: You mean Eileen?

Another pause - then -

TYRONE: (*almost sadly*) Yeah... I guess I do.

SISTER MIRIAM: That's wonderful, Mr Kane. Congratulations. (*gently*) You love her, don't you?

Tyrone hesitates, then -

TYRONE: I suppose so...But in a different way to Jean - that was my wife.

SISTER MIRIAM: Yes.

TYRONE: What I felt for Jean won't happen again. (*sad smile*) It was one of those - freaks of nature - like Niagara Falls or the Grand Canyon. But if I let that love destroy me, then all the good from Jean will be gone - and all the bad things in life will have won. (*with rare honesty*) So I'm going on. And I'm not looking back.

TYRONE: (*more optimistically*) Eileen's kind - and she's loyal - and she cares about things. She even wants to save the world - which is fine by me - we all need hobbies.

SISTER MIRIAM: (*returning the engagement ring*) Here's your ring. I'm sure she'll adore it.

TYRONE: Sister Miriam - the reason I'm here is - well - I don't know how to ask her...I need some advice.

SISTER MIRIAM: What words did you use with Jean?

TYRONE: That was easy. I just said - (*without much enthusiasm*) "All right." ...
So I'm going to need some practice. (*nervously*) Do you mind if I borrow your hand, Sister Miriam?

SISTER MIRIAM: I really don't think I -

TYRONE: (*desperate*) Go on. Be a sport. Just pretend you're Eileen.

SISTER MIRIAM: She's a communist!

TYRONE: Work with me. Please.

SISTER MIRIAM: All right.

And Sister Miriam removes the drawer - and slips her hand through the grille.

Tyrone, of course, cannot see her face, just her hand.

SISTER MIRIAM: You are kneeling, aren't you? Every woman wants that.

And Tyrone kneels.

TYRONE: (*nervously taking Sister Miriam 's hand*) I've known you now for over a year. Well - sure - I'm a drunk - but you're not getting any younger.

SISTER MIRIAM: Mr Kane!!

TYRONE: Ssshhh. I'm on a roll!!

And Tyrone looks at Sister Miriam's hand again.

TYRONE: The smart thing to do is to pool our resources - become a team. I've wasted too much of my life already. It's time to seize the day.

Now Tyrone takes her hand.

TYRONE: (*very sincerely*) I'll give you my body - what's left of it, my heart - for what it's worth - and my soul, which may or may not exist. And all I ask in return is to see in me what you saw at the start: someone you could believe in. And I'll do my best to live up to that belief. Forever and ever.

(*gently*) "The one great enterprise in this world - is to learn how to love and keep loving."

(*to Sister Miriam*) The poet wrote that. The dead one you like.

SISTER MIRIAM: (*trying not to cry*) Did he now?

And Sister Miriam looks at the grille, amazed, and overcome.

For the first time since her husband's death, she would actually like to live.

SISTER MIRIAM: (*pulling her hand away gently*) I'm sure she'll think that's very nice. Any woman would. (*rising quickly but unsteadily*) I have to go.

TYRONE: Sister - wait - please -

SISTER MIRIAM: (*shocked at her own feelings*) Mr Kane - whatever you're thinking - don't say it!

TYRONE: (*slightly surprised*) But I was thinking I'd like my ring back.

And Sister Miriam looks at her hand - and realises she is still wearing it..

Darkness. On the soundtrack we hear Mary O'Hara singing **Where Will the Wedding Be?** *from* **The Frog's Wedding***.*

SCENE TWENTY-TWO

Mother Raphael is clutching a telescope and looking at something outside.

Sister Miriam is nearby.

MOTHER RAPHAEL: Anselma was right. This is fascinating.

SISTER MIRIAM: (*fondly*) Dear old thing. She loved her astronomy. It's what she missed most when she went blind.

MOTHER RAPHAEL: (*focusing the telescope*) Astronomy? Hah! She didn't know a comet from a kidney bean. Before she died she confessed to me that she used this to look at the Hampstead Drive-In. And by golly she was right! You can see it from here. Both screens.

MOTHER RAPHAEL (*casually, as she peers through the telescope*) I just wonder where we'll bury her.

SISTER MIRIAM: She has a grave.

MOTHER RAPHAEL: Not since they put our telephone cable there.

Sister Miriam hesitates - and then says - calmly -

SISTER MIRIAM: Then I'd like her to have mine, Mother.

MOTHER RAPHAEL: (*turns, surprised*) Yours?

SISTER MIRIAM: It's quiet - and sunny - and faces the Drive In.

MOTHER RAPHAEL: Both screens?

SISTER MIRIAM: Yes.

MOTHER RAPHAEL: (*not objecting, just curious*) And where will you be buried?

SISTER MIRIAM: Where I belong. Next to Richard.

MOTHER RAPHAEL: I see. (*casually*) Your father sent you a letter today. He says that your records are selling extremely well.

SISTER MIRIAM: (*secretly pleased*) I didn't think people liked folk songs now.

MOTHER RAPHAEL: Maybe it's you they like. (*peering through telescope at Drive In screen*) Holy moly! I hope those two are married! Oh - gosh - now they're doing it. (*It*) Makes you miss it much more when you actually see it.

SISTER MIRIAM: (*if she's shocked, she hides it*) See what, Mother?

MOTHER RAPHAEL: Smoking. I'd kill for a Craven-A Cork Tip. (*looking at Sister Miriam*) What about you? What do you miss?

SISTER MIRIAM: Mascara. Before I joined the convent, the Bishop said I had to go six weeks without make-up.

MOTHER RAPHAEL: Trust a man to do that!

SISTER MIRIAM: (*gently, calmly*) Mother - I would like to see my face again.

Mother Raphael knows just what this implies - that Sister Miriam is thinking of leaving the Order - but her reply is also calm.

MOTHER RAPHAEL: And what's brought on this - sudden urge?

SISTER MIRIAM: I'm not sure. It isn't vanity - I don't care what I look like. (*hesitates, then*)
But I think - I think I finally understand love. And the proper thing to do for Richard is for me to go on with my life...So it's time I resurrected her - Mary O'Hara, I mean. And I'd just like to see how she's weathered these years.

MOTHER RAPHAEL: You won't be disappointed. (*removing a small purse mirror from under the bed*) I think - Sister Miriam - that when the time comes you should use a little lipstick - and lots and lots of curlers. I'm not sure what they're wearing in the world, but from what I've glimpsed in The Catholic Weekly you're in for a few surprises. (*passing the mirror to Sister Miriam*) I used this when Anselma was dying. When her breath left the glass, I knew she had gone. Still - a Sister never really leaves us. I shall ring the Decca people tomorrow.

SISTER MIRIAM: But -

MOTHER RAPHAEL: No backing down.

Then Mother Raphael blesses Sister Miriam - and as she exits mutters -

MOTHER RAPHAEL: And no peeking at the Drive In.

Sister Miriam reaches out, nervously, and picks up the small mirror.

At first she hesitates, then she holds it up to look at her face for the first time in 13 years.

At first there is no re-action. She could be looking at a stranger. Then she looks closer, touches her face, realises it is herself, smiles nervously, laughs and then - mid-laugh - begins to weep gently but happily - as one does when one meets an old friend unexpectedly.

SCENE TWENTY-THREE

We see a sign that says: 129 Abbey Road London.

Traffic noises are followed by the sound of an electric buzzer. It rings two or three times.

The lights come up to reveal Mother Raphael alone on stage, the harp beside her. Mother Raphael is standing in front of a small security grille - which is attached to the (unseen) front door of Decca Records.

Mother Raphael is speaking to an unseen and impersonal Security Guard.

SECURITY GUARD: (Voice Only) Decca Records.

Mother Raphael looks around, slightly puzzled, then realises that the Voice is coming from the grille.

MOTHER RAPHAEL: Are you the Commissionaire?

SECURITY GUARD: (Voice Only) I'm Security, m'am.

MOTHER RAPHAEL: (*flustered but hiding it*) Oh. Well the front door's jammed.

SECURITY GUARD: (Voice Only) Will you talk into the grille please?

MOTHER RAPHAEL: (*loudly, slowly into the grille*) Open - the - door!

SECURITY GUARD: (Voice Only) No - can - do.

MOTHER RAPHAEL: And why not?

SECURITY GUARD: (Voice Only) As if you didn't know. I've been ordered to keep all groupies out until Mick Jagger's gone.

MOTHER RAPHAEL: Groupies?

SECURITY GUARD: (Voice Only) Some chicks 'll do anything to get near the Stones. Well it's not gonna work, darling. So bugger off - or I'll send out the "muscle". And next time rent a costume that fits.

Sister Miriam, meanwhile, walks over and joins her Superior

SECURITY GUARD: (*sees Sister Miriam and is suddenly a lot more affable*) Why didn't you tell me that you'd brought a friend. My shift ends at noon - and I'm "into" threesomes.

SISTER MIRIAM: (*delighted to hear his voice, talks into the grille*) Rodney Whitehead - is that really you? Does your wife still sew for the Children of Mary?

A horrified pause - then -

SECURITY GUARD: (Voice Only) (*in disbelief*) Miss O'Hara? (*alarmed whisper*) Miss O'Hara?

And the door goes "buzz" - and opens. Mary O'Hara is back at Decca.

SCENE TWENTY-FOUR

A large red sign proclaims : Silence! Recording.

Sister Miriam is practising scales - trying to find her voice under very stressful conditions.

MOTHER RAPHAEL: They want to know when you'll start.

SISTER MIRIAM: (*her hands are shaking*) As soon as they stop staring. You'd think they'd never seen a nun.

MOTHER RAPHAEL: Most of them haven't. Even that Mick Jagger came in for a look when you were recording the harp music. I'm not sure what he does exactly - but the poor man's lips are enormous. Perhaps he's a flautist.

Suddenly an unseen Male Voice (a Decca Sound Engineer) calls out from the Recording Area.

SOUND ENGINEER: (Voice Only) Can we get a move on please?

SISTER MIRIAM: (*calmly but desperately*) Mother - I'm scared.

MOTHER RAPHAEL: (*calmly also*) So am I. But God isn't. And that's all that matters.

SOUND ENGINEER: (Voice Only) (impatiently) Let's not turn this into "The Sound of Music". "The Grateful Dead" want to use the studio!

MOTHER RAPHAEL: Even their dead are impatient now. (*blesses Sister Miriam softly but with great intensity*) The best hour of the day be thine, Sister Miriam.

And Mother Raphael exits.

*Sister Miriam is alone in the studio. She looks at the microphone, hesitates, then begins to sing **Danny Boy** - the ultimate song of love and loss - accompanied by the harp music she recorded earlier at the Decca studios.*

And as she sings it , Sister Miriam's seventeen years of grieving for Richard Selig come to an end.

SCENE TWENTY-FIVE

Tyrone is standing at the Visitors' Grille, ringing the bell impatiently. He is wearing a very nice suit.

TYRONE: (*rings*) Sister Miriam? Sister Miriam? (*mutters loudly*) Come on, woman. Move those feet!

And Sister Miriam enters. She walks - almost strolls - calmly and slowly - towards the grille.

SISTER MIRIAM: Who's there please?

TYRONE: You know damn well who it is! Even Saint Walburga could smell all this Brut.

SISTER MIRIAM: Mr Kane? Has a fire broken out?

TYRONE: I happen to be running late. (*proudly*) I'm on my way to Heathrow.

SISTER MIRIAM: Heathrow?

TYRONE: It's an airport!

SISTER MIRIAM: I'm aware of that. (*surprised*) Are you flying somewhere?

TYRONE: Back home. Eileen's waiting in the car.

SISTER MIRIAM: Then bring her in - by all means!

TYRONE: I tried. But she won't budge. She used to be a Tyke, you see. And she thinks if she sets foot in here, God'll strike her dead. (*pauses, grins*) I made an honest woman of her at the Workers' Club last night. (*brief pause*) We're married, Sister Miriam.

If Sister Miriam has any disappointments, she hides them.

SISTER MIRIAM: Oh - Mr Kane - that's wonderful!

TYRONE: The big tough "commies " howled all through the ceremony.

Tyrone leans close to the grille - then says in a confidential tone -

TYRONE: To tell you the truth, she's got "a bun in the oven". Typical Catholic. I think they're born pregnant!

SISTER MIRIAM: (*smiles*) You'll be a father after all.

TYRONE: Yeah. No more "pram ache". Oh - here - (*reaches into his pocket, takes out something and puts it in the grille's drawer*) - for you.

SISTER MIRIAM: (*taking it from the drawer*) What's this then?

TYRONE: Wedding cake. (*teasing*)

TYRONE: You know what they say. Put it under your pillow and you'll dream about your husband!

SISTER MIRIAM: So what will you live on - in America?

TYRONE: I thought I might sell leaf cards.

SISTER MIRIAM: Mr Kane!

TYRONE: Only joking... (*hesitates, then*) I used to be a doctor.

SISTER MIRIAM: You?

TYRONE: Yeah...So I'm going back to my old job. I'd be crazy not to - I've got a free receptionist in the car. (*sniffs*) What's that smell? It's not my Brut.

SISTER MIRIAM: (*nervously*) No. I think it must be me.

TYRONE: (*puzzled*) You?

SISTER MIRIAM: (*defensive*) Yes. Why?

TYRONE: (*surprised*) It's nice.

SISTER MIRIAM: Really? It's Evening in Paris. A perfume.

TYRONE: I didn't think you penguins could wear that stuff.

SISTER MIRIAM: Sometimes we do. This is a gift - from all the Sisters- (*hesitates*) - a going-away present. I'm leaving too.

TYRONE: (*astonished*) Leaving Stanbrook?

SISTER MIRIAM: (*calmly, casually*) Yes.

Tyrone is almost lost for words. He wonders if she's telling him the whole truth.

TYRONE: Oh...Oh...Well I hope you like your new convent. Same brand of nuns is it? I mean how do I write to you?

SISTER MIRIAM: I don't have the address yet. But you can send your letters here.

TYRONE: (*suspicious*) Is everything all right?

SISTER MIRIAM: Why shouldn't it be?

TYRONE: I worry about you sometimes. I think you're like the Communists. You're not as tough as you sound.

SISTER MIRIAM: You really should hurry or -

TYRONE: You wouldn't believe what doctors earn in New York - especially those who treat alcoholics. (*gently*) So you can hit me for money any time you want - doesn't matter what it's for - a new whip - a hair- shirt . Just pick up the phone - and it's yours.

SISTER MIRIAM: (*touched*) That's very kind of you, Mr Kane.

TYRONE: Well - in return I expect you to pray for me. I mean a lot could go wrong.

SISTER MIRIAM: But it won't.

TYRONE: No. It won't....I know I should say "thanks". But it's an over-used word. Like "love". Every so often you try to load it with all the meaning you can. And it's still not enough.

SISTER MIRIAM: Don't worry then.

TYRONE: OK...Look - the first time I came here - I remember being drunk and - well - did I imagine it or did you somehow know I was from the Bronx?

SISTER MIRIAM: I knew.

TYRONE: How?

A pause, then -

SISTER MIRIAM: (*calmly*) I was married once, Mr Kane. To an American.

TYRONE: (*stunned*) But you're a nun.

SISTER MIRIAM: It was before I joined the convent.

TYRONE: (*realises what's been happening*) Then he's -

SISTER MIRIAM: (*calmly*) I'm a widow. Yes.

TYRONE: Oh. Oh - shoot - shoot - me and my big mouth. I'm so -

SISTER MIRIAM: It's quite all right. I've come to terms with it. Now you go on. You musn't keep Eileen waiting.

TYRONE: Bit of sun will do her good.

Suddenly Tyrone doesn't want to leave.

TYRONE: (*nervously*) I don't suppose I could see you - your face I mean. Just this once.

SISTER MIRIAM: (*gently*) It's not allowed.

TYRONE: But it seems so strange - not coming here again. No more leaf-cards - or manure - or you throwing things at me...How do you say goodbye to a nun?

SISTER MIRIAM: Well - you put your palms against the grille - right here -

She taps two positions in front of her, on her side of the grille.

TYRONE: (*whispers gently, lovingly*) OK.

SISTER MIRIAM: - and I put mine against yours.

Tyrone kneels and places his palms in front of him, against the
   grille.

On the other side of the grille Sister Miriam is kneeling also,
   facing him, with her palms on his. They cannot see each
   other.

TYRONE: (*tenderly*) Who'd have thought that both of us would
   end up smelling nice?

SISTER MIRIAM: (*tenderly also*) Yes. Isn't that a co-
   incidence?

A pause - then -

TYRONE: Goodbye, Sister Miriam.

SISTER MIRIAM: Goodbye, Doctor Kane.

They remain kneeling like this for about twenty seconds as the
   chapel's bell tolls gently in the distance.

Gradual darkness... And on screen we see a billboard
   proclaiming:
Carnegie Hall - 8.30pm - Mary O'Hara Returns to her Music! A
   Sold Out sticker has been placed across it.

We also see photos of Mary O'Hara playing the harp on stage.

And at the same time we hear the Voice of the real Mary O'Hara
   during this concert. As the audience applauds she
   introduces one of the songs that made her want to sing
   *again - **Lord of the Dance**. And she sings two verses from*
   it.

SCENE TWENTY-SIX

On the screen we see the words Three Years Later.

Mother Raphael is sitting behind the grille in the Visitors' Area at Stanbrook Abbey. Since there's no one around, Mother Raphael is puffing on a Craven A Cork Tip cigarette and enjoying it immensely.

Then the door opens and a smartly-dressed and attractive woman enters, stands still - then simply looks around. The woman is Mary O'Hara.

MOTHER RAPHAEL: Hello? Is someone there?

Mary O'Hara recognizes the voice behind the grille and smiles.

MOTHER RAPHAEL: (*slightly impatient*) You have to speak into the grille. Over here.

MARY O'HARA: But I -

MOTHER RAPHAEL: And to save you the trouble of asking why, this convent is enclosed. Our contact with the world is strictly limited to those who need our help.

MARY O'HARA: But what about your family - and friends? Surely they're allowed to visit and have a little chat.

MOTHER RAPHAEL: Not anymore. Like it or lump it, those are the rules. And our new bishop's strict. No excuses. No exceptions.

MARY O'HARA: (*trying to hide her disappointment*) Yes. Of course. I understand.

MOTHER RAPHAEL: Well - you're way ahead of most of our guests. Now what can I do for you? No - let me guess - you missed the turn-off to London?

MARY O'HARA: That's right. I was on my way to a concert.

MOTHER RAPHAEL: Go back half a mile - then head east - towards the drive in.

MARY O'HARA: Thank you. (*sniffs*) Is that a Craven-A Cork Tip?

MOTHER RAPHAEL: (*putting the cigarette out quickly*) No. It's incense.

Then a pause - because Mother Raphael is starting to suspect who her visitor is.

MOTHER RAPHAEL: (*sniffs*) Is that Evening in Paris?

MARY O'HARA: Yes. Some dear friends gave it to me.

MOTHER RAPHAEL: Perhaps you'd like to buy something from the rack by the window.

MARY O'HARA: What would you recommend?

MOTHER RAPHAEL: Why not take a leaf-card? (*with great tenderness*) They were made by one of our Sisters - who is greatly loved - and missed by all.

MARY O'HARA: (*touched*) I'm sure she'd be pleased to know that.

And Mary places some money in the small Money Box.

MOTHER RAPHAEL: (*hearing the rattle of the coins*) Thank you - I didn't catch your name, Miss -

MARY O'HARA: It's Mrs - Mrs O'Toole. I was married last year. (*whispers it with gratitude*) We're very happy.

Mother Raphael struggles to hide her delight .

MOTHER RAPHAEL: (*calmly*) Are you indeed. How nice for you. Have a safe trip to London, Mrs O'Toole. The best hour of the day be thine.

MARY O'HARA: Thank you. (*touching the grille with her palm*) Thank you very much.

Mary O'Hara heads for the door, turns, has one last look and leaves.

As soon as Mother Raphael hears the door shut, she calls out -

MOTHER RAPHAEL: (*excitedly*) Sister Walburga! Sister Walburga! I've just had some wonderful news. You'd better get out the brandy. That's right - the brandy. Well don't just stand there. Bring a glass for yourself . A great big glass. (*with real enjoyment*) And bugger the bishop!

*On the soundtrack Mary O'Hara sings **Lord of the Dance** joyfully.*

At the same time we hear the clinking of glasses. Mother Raphael is pouring herself a medicinal brandy. She deserves it.

THE END

OTHER TITLES AVAILABLE FROM ORiGiN™ THEATRICAL

DARK VOYAGER
John Misto

Hollywood, 1962. Bette Davis and Joan Crawford are at war. Between them they've terrorized movie studios for over three decades, married nine husbands, made two hundred films and guzzled enough booze to fill the Hoover Dam. Now their careers are on the skids and Bette and Joan are locked in a titanic struggle for top-billing on their latest movie.

When America's most feared columnist, Hedda Hopper, invites them to supper, they call an uneasy truce. But the evening turns chaotic when an unexpected guest arrives -- Marilyn Monroe, drunk, drugged, dishevelled, the face of "new" Hollywood. Soon Marilyn is drawn into the Davis-Crawford war, and what begins as a game becomes a battle for survival. Will old age and treachery defeat youth and courage? Or is there more to Marilyn Monroe than anyone could have guessed?

You are cordially invited to join these legendary ladies for the ultimate show-biz meal. It has a menu with something to appeal to everyone: singing, dancing, party-games... and just a bit of murder.

"John Misto taps into something pretty much universal, the passion, more to the point obsession that people have with everything to do with celebrity." - Sydney Arts Guide

Casting: 1M, 4F
Full Length Play, Dark Comedy, 1960s

www.origintheatrical.com.au

127

.

www.ingramcontent.com/pod-product-compliance
Lightning Source LLC
Chambersburg PA
CBHW072200090426
42740CB00012B/2326